A volume in the series

MASTERS of MODERN LANDSCAPE DESIGN

LALH

Library of American Landscape History

ROBERT ROYSTON

REUBEN M. RAINEY
AND JC MILLER

THE UNIVERSITY OF GEORGIA PRESS
ATHENS

LIBRARY OF AMERICAN LANDSCAPE HISTORY
AMHERST, MASSACHUSETTS

Publication of this book was made possible in part through a grant from the Bruce and Georgia McEver Fund for the Arts and Environment.

Published by the University of Georgia Press
www.ugapress.org
in association with Library of American Landscape History
www.lalh.org
Copyright © 2020 by Library of American Landscape History
All rights reserved

Designed and typeset by Jonathan D. Lippincott
Set in Bembo

The paper in this book meets the guidelines for permanence and durability of the Committee on Production Guidelines for Book Longevity of the Council on Library Resources.

Most University of Georgia Press titles are available from popular e-book vendors.

Printed in South Korea through
Four Colour Print Group, Louisville, Kentucky

19 20 21 22 23 P 5 4 3 2 1

Library of Congress Cataloging-in-Publication Data
Names: Rainey, Reuben M., author. | Miller, J. C.
(Landscape architect), author.
Title: Robert Royston / Reuben M. Rainey and JC Miller.
Description: Athens : The University of Georgia Press, [2019] |
Series: Masters of modern landscape design | Includes
bibliographical references and index.
Identifiers: LCCN 2019030460 | ISBN 9780820357317 (paperback)
Subjects: LCSH: Royston, Robert, 1918–2008. | Landscape architects—
United States—Biography. | California—Biography.
Classification: LCC SB470.R69 R355 2020 | DDC 712.092 [B]—dc23
LC record available at https://lccn.loc.gov/2019030460

Frontispiece: Robert Royston, late 1960s. Collection of JC Miller.

VOLUME FUNDERS

Hubbard Educational Foundation

Foundation for Landscape Studies

Nancy G. Frederick

Thomas Lemann / Parkside Foundation

Janine Luke
Friedrike Merck
Wendy and David Barensfeld Family Charitable Fund

David Kamp, FASLA
Ann Mullins, FASLA / Margaret A. Frank Fund at The
    Chicago Community Foundation
Nancy Newcomb and John Hargraves
Peter Pennoyer Architects
G. P. Schafer Architect
Margaret D. Sullivan
Andre Tchelistcheff

Karen Bartholomew
Josephine Bush
Ann Cicarella
Madison Cox
George W. Curry, FASLA
Elisabeth French

Lisa Gimmy, ASLA, LEED AP
Esley Hamilton
Heidi Hohmann, ASLA
Manuela King
Francis R. Kowsky
Margaret Jean McKee
Scot Medbury
Darwina Neal, FASLA
Jon Powell, ASLA, and Jeri Deneen
Nancy B. Taylor
Brian Tichenor
Peter Walker, FASLA

CONTENTS

PREFACE

Robert Royston (1918–2007) has long been overshadowed by his colleagues Dan Kiley, Garrett Eckbo, and James Rose, whose raucous writings overturned the Beaux-Arts landscape design methods taught at Harvard's Graduate School of Design in the late 1930s. But Royston was no less a maverick than his better-known contemporaries. His focus on spatial composition as a dominant component of landscape design was more emphatic than any other practitioner's of his day. For Royston, the perception of space was based in the senses and, ultimately, its impact was emotional: "Wherever you are, look around, feel it," he wrote. "How does the space affect your mind and body, how does it play with your senses? What are you seeing? What are the sounds? The smells? What are you physically touching? How many cultural connections or memories are suggested? What is the emotional response?"

Royston's impact on the field of American landscape

design was notable owing to both his prodigious output (nearly two thousand projects over his long career) and his successful reinvigoration of small parks and playgrounds as agents of social change. His most lasting legacy can be seen in the Bay Area, where he maintained a practice through various iterations of his office for more than six decades. Royston designed parks and playgrounds as elements of open space networks—in his words, the "landscape matrix": in essence, a series of linked public spaces that would serve a broad range of visitors and thereby address urgent urban planning issues in a region undergoing explosive development. Royston approached the design of small parks much as he did his private gardens, with an emphasis on fine detail, comfort, and beauty. Enlivened by shapes and rhythms inspired by modern painting and sculpture, his playgrounds in particular broke new ground. Children gravitated to the imaginative abstract forms for tunneling and climbing and the opportunity to drive "grown-up" pedal cars or inhabit "apartment" towers.

In determining which of Royston's built work to cover in their text, the authors opted to address a broad spectrum of landscape types. So in addition to Royston's more familiar parks and playgrounds, readers will find discussions of residential landscapes (including Royston's last garden, designed in 2007); college campuses; cemeteries; housing developments; and, most unusual, the cover of a water reservoir in Piedmont, California, arguably Royston's most explicit expression of abstraction in landscape design.

The fourth volume in the series Masters of Modern Landscape Design, *Robert Royston* continues our exploration of midcentury landscape design, from gardens to national parks. I am grateful to Reuben Rainey and JC Miller for their excellent work on this book and to the team of editors who assisted in the task, especially Sarah Allaback and Carol Betsch. My thanks go to Mary Bellino for her fine index and editorial acumen and to Jonathan Lippincott for his sleek design. I thank the Hubbard Educational Foundation and the Foundation for Landscape Studies for their generous support and the many individual donors whose generosity also made this volume possible.

Robin Karson
Executive Director
Library of American Landscape History

ACKNOWLEDGMENTS

The authors are grateful for the generous and indispensable support of many individuals and organizations. During the last decade of his life, Robert Royston provided autobiographical reflections as well as slides and drawings from his private collection. He accompanied us on field trips to some of his major parks and assisted us on our visits to the Environmental Design Archives at the University of California, Berkeley. There he sifted through numerous stacks of his drawings and those of his partners, explaining their design intentions. His strong support and frequent availability provided us with a vivid and enduring understanding of the profound humanism of his design values, the enthusiasm and optimism informing his many projects, and the large scope of his professional achievements.

We were able to provide the extensive graphic representation that Royston's work deserves through a generous

David R. Coffin Publication Grant from the Foundation for Landscape Studies.

Royston's partners in RHBA and RHAA, Harold Kobayashi, Louis Alley, and Eldon Beck, provided valuable insights into the firm's method of team design and background details of several major projects. Waverly Lowell, curator (now retired), and the staff at the Environmental Design Archives helped us mine the riches of the Royston/RHAA Collection. The library staff of Stanford University helped uncover valuable materials on the Stanford Linear Accelerator Project. Kenneth Helphand provided his personal slides of the early phases of the Sunriver project, which substantially aided our analysis. Marc Treib accompanied us on several field trips and provided valuable commentary on Royston's work. Hannelore Royston allowed us frequent access to the Royston house in Mill Valley, which greatly assisted our case study of that work.

Sarah Allaback was the consummate editor: insightful, demanding, helpful, and patient. She kept our work on track and encouraged a clarity and succinctness that much improved the final text. Carol Betsch's excellent copy editing and assistance with illustration selection was much appreciated, as was Jonathan Lippincott's fine talent as a graphic designer. Sue Rainey drew upon her early career as an editor and patiently and effectively critiqued numerous drafts as well.

Finally, we greatly appreciate the invitation of Robin Karson, executive director of the Library of American Landscape History, to coauthor this volume for the LALH Masters of Modern Landscape Design series.

ROBERT ROYSTON

Fig. 1. Santa Clara Central Park, picnic pavilion, 2018. Photo by Tom Fitzgerald.

OVERVIEW

One bright spring day in 2005, we accompanied Robert Royston on his first visit to Santa Clara Central Park in more than three decades. He was eager to see if the largest and most elaborate of his public parks remained as he remembered. Sporting a jaunty straw hat and self-designed bolo tie, Royston traversed the fifty-two-acre park from end to end with a swiftness and agility belying his eighty-seven years. Finding the park little changed from his original design, he enthusiastically explained how its major features—a huge umbrella-like picnic pavilion, an imaginative children's playground fashioned from recycled quarry stones, and an elaborate planting plan with clusters of giant redwoods— were tailored to the needs of various age groups, from toddlers to the elderly (fig. 1).

Royston most enjoyed greeting visitors with a broad smile and asking them what they thought about the park. Whether the recipient of his friendly inquiry was a child, teenager, or adult, the response was always positive. The park's engaging playgrounds, well-designed facilities for croquet and field sports, and welcoming spaces for social gatherings were among many features recalled with pleasure. Royston's ad hoc survey was not a rigorous analysis, yet we heard similar expressions of gratitude when interviewing visitors in five other Bay Area parks he designed.[1] During our trip to Santa Clara's Central Park, one woman seated on a bench with her husband quipped, "I would not marry him unless he promised me we would live near this park." It was a fitting tribute to a landscape architect who had designed over a hundred and fifty urban parks and plazas in the Bay Area alone—landscapes that reflected his vision of a humane and vibrant civic realm.

First in a small studio and later as the director of large, interdisciplinary firms, Robert Royston played a role in more than two thousand projects—from private gardens, parks, and school grounds to new towns, regional landscape plans, and transit corridors. His prodigious output reflects the changing dynamics of his profession as well as his significant influence on the development of the postwar landscape architecture firm into a highly specialized corporation. The lasting footprint of Royston's accomplishments is most apparent in the Bay Area, where he and his colleagues enhanced the civic infrastructure of dozens of towns, but he also designed landscapes in Salt Lake City, New Orleans, Portland, Oregon, St. Louis, Aspen, and Reno, and took on international projects in Venezuela, Chile, Mexico, Taiwan, Singapore, Malaysia, the Philippines, and Canada. The high quality and range of his work, combined with its sheer volume, substantiate his reputation as a leading modernist landscape architect of the mid-twentieth century.

Royston began his career working for Thomas Church, one of the country's most prominent modernist garden designers, in a firm at the forefront of a profession undergoing unprecedented change. By the late 1940s, postwar prosperity, advances in technology, and a surge in population had led to the development of new building types demanding new landscapes, as well as a design methodology appropriate to the times. Royston left Church to join the next generation of modernist practitioners. In his partnership with Garrett Eckbo and Edward Williams (1945–1958), he produced some of his most outstanding residential work—plans that illustrate his attention to detail, sensitive approach to design, and skill in manipulating space. The dramatic arcs, stacked grids, and amoeba-like forms characteristic of the modernist style were put to practical use, as Royston created engaging, functional spaces for outdoor living. His gardens were carefully choreographed to his clients' lifestyles, but he also strove for a sense of timelessness in his design (fig. 2). Within five years, Eckbo, Royston & Williams had become one of the nation's leading modernist landscape architectural firms.

Royston's experience with private gardens informed his early public park designs, which evolved into his conception of a new type of park for the American family. His unique approach to planning parks involved envisioning a series of linked "public gardens" that would serve a broad range of visitors and could be adapted to a variety of settings, from small neighborhoods to large cities. Through these park designs—residential gardens writ large—Royston also addressed pressing issues of urban planning in a region undergoing the stress of intense development. In addition to drawing on modernist theory and avant-garde art, he incorporated technical information from government booklets that provided recommendations for the sizes of parks in any

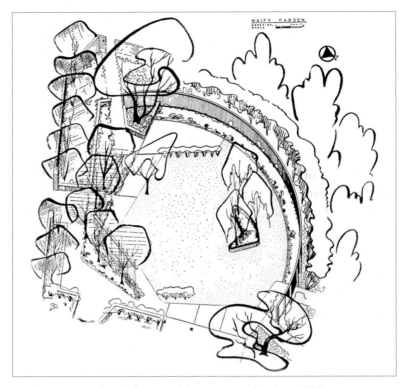

Fig. 2. Naify garden, Atherton, CA, isometric drawing, 1952. Robert N. Royston Collection, Environmental Design Archives, UC Berkeley (RC EDA).

given area and practical standards for their implementation. Meeting the basic needs of visitors and creating parks that could withstand increased urban growth—priorities that other modernist landscape architects sometimes neglected—became central to his design methodology. Royston tempered this utilitarian approach with his command of an elegant and visually engaging artistic style, and the balance of the two revolutionized public park design.

In 1958, Royston left Eckbo and Williams to launch his own firm, building on the collaborative, interdisciplinary model of their partnership, with Asa Hanamoto and David

R. Mayes. Joined soon after by Eldon Beck, the team quickly established itself by acquiring commissions for Bowden Park in Palo Alto (1960) and Central Park in Santa Clara (1963). These were particularly meaningful commissions for Royston, who saw his gardens and parks as contributions to the larger framework of urban and suburban planning (fig. 3). Like his modernist peers, he regarded space as the primary medium of his profession and respected the intrinsic qualities of materials. His use of plants emphasized their role in defining space and contributing to the multisensual dimension of spatial experience, especially color, texture, and scent. His formal vocabulary was influenced by twentieth-century painting and

Fig. 3. Bowden Park, Palo Alto, 1961. Collection of JC Miller (JCM).

sculpture, and he strove to create environments suitable for modern living. But when he considered space, he also looked beyond the elite design world, with its one-sided emphasis on form for form's sake, to the suburban sprawl creeping its way into the Bay Area. Not content to watch this growth go unchecked, he became an activist for better urban planning.

In 1961, Royston narrated and produced a short documentary film, *A Community Park,* in which he introduced a new kind of park aimed at the needs of the family.[2] His model plan was a response to the rapid construction of suburban tract homes—built too quickly and too close together. In many of these subdivisions, the street was the only open space for children's play. Footage of girls sitting on a curb, boys playing in the street, and teenagers congregating on a street corner documented this reality. Although he understood that citizens were helpless to stop suburban sprawl, Royston urged them to "insist on space, acquire land, plan a park." The documentary was filmed in Palo Alto at Mitchell Park, which Royston had designed five years earlier, but the site was not identified. Rather, it served as an example of the kind of place that communities should demand, and the film was an example of the public engagement and social activism Royston advocated as crucial to the development of a safe and sane suburban environment. By the end of his career, his park work would include commissions in seven western states and Malaysia, Canada, and Australia. In collaboration with colleagues from his San Francisco and Mill Valley offices, he was involved in the design of nine national parks, fourteen regional parks, and 109 city and community parks.

During the mid-1970s, the firm, now Royston, Hanamoto, Beck & (Kazuo) Abey, grew to include six principals, four associates, and specialists in regional and urban planning, architecture, forestry, and business management. Bolstered by sustained economic growth and new government programs, the firm would help to manage the steadily increasing development of the Bay Area and work to lessen its impact on the environment. In the nearly forty years he led and continued to expand his firm, Royston spread his influence to generations of designers, some of whom went on to establish their own successful firms and others, like his former student Asa Hanamoto, who stayed with him for their entire careers. The longevity of his practice attests to the forward-looking nature of his vision, his optimistic outlook, and his ability to inspire colleagues, clients, and the general public. Today the firm of Royston, Hanamoto, (Louis) Alley & Abey (RHAA) continues to honor Royston's philosophy by emphasizing the importance of collaboration in the effort to design "for the human experience."[3]

Throughout his career, Royston made an extraordinary effort to understand the needs of his clients—regardless of age, class, or gender. His projects manipulate space and form to achieve both practical ends, such as comfortable seating, and more spiritual purposes, like the joy evoked by playful

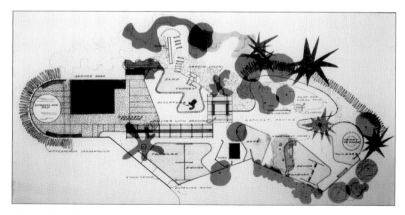

Fig. 4. Pixie Place, Ross, CA, plan, n.d. JCM.

sculpture or the serenity of a stroll beneath blooming trees (fig. 4). An imaginative and empathetic designer, Royston considered the psychological effects of space and materials—as much as their visual and technical aspects—and adjusted his designs to the benefit of all. His perceptive humanism, woven into five decades of professional practice, is his enduring legacy.

Robert Norman Royston was born in San Francisco on April 25, 1918.[4] His parents, Walter and Doris, moved to a ranch near the small market town of Morgan Hill in Northern California's Santa Clara Valley when Royston was six. Walter, a retired mechanical and electrical engineer wishing to remain active, purchased a twenty-acre walnut ranch, and Royston and his siblings, an older brother and a younger sister, were part of the demanding day-to-day work routine. Young Royston's experience of the ranch, with its efficient site plan and utilitarian buildings, shaped his perspective on nature and sparked his interest in gardening and city planning. As an eight-year-old, completely on his own initiative, Royston designed a small vegetable garden and sold its produce to his mother. Two years later, inspired by a family trip to Santa Barbara, he created an elaborate model of this "ideal city" with buildings of compressed earth sited on a twenty-by-forty-foot plot and arranged on a grid of streets. Late in his life he remarked on this portent of his future professional career with a laugh and said he had constructed the model not only because Santa Barbara impressed him but because "it was the first time I realized there were cities out there other than Morgan Hill."[5]

During his high school years Royston pursued an unusually diverse assortment of interests. He discovered a talent for drawing, competed in basketball and track, and enjoyed acting in school plays. One teacher, recognizing his combination of physical grace and verbal fluency, advised him to become a lawyer or ballet dancer.[6] In his senior year, he came across the major "Landscape Design" in the University of California course catalog and became intrigued by a discipline that combined his interest in drama, agriculture, art, and outdoor activities. A trip to Berkeley for an interview with the program's founder and chair, John W. Gregg, confirmed his expectations. He vividly recalled the interview: "It was a high-ceilinged room with the books around and a very nice, considerate old gentleman, and he asked me lots of questions about what I liked to do. I said I was very interested in the theater and I was torn between the theater and landscape architecture. But I loved to draw and paint and so on, and I liked the outdoors. And that's how it happened. So he opened all the doors."[7]

Fresh off the farm, Royston was fortunate to have chosen a program in the School of Agriculture that considered landscape architecture a blend of natural science and fine art. As chair of the Landscape Design division, Gregg had developed a curriculum shaped by his mentor, Frank A. Waugh of Massachusetts Agricultural College (now University of Massachusetts Amherst). Students were required to take twenty-seven units in studio art and architecture, six in botany, and three in civil engineering, as well as landscape design courses.[8]

Royston attended UC Berkeley from 1936 to 1940, during the aftermath of the Great Depression and the increasing threat of World War II, a period of transition for both the economy of the Bay Area and the profession of landscape architecture. Since the collapse of the stock market, lucrative commissions for large estate gardens had steadily diminished, but FDR's New Deal public works programs, along with the expanded National Park Service, provided commissions for state park site plans, low-cost housing, and parkway construction that fended off economic disaster for many firms.[9] The shift in the profession was also ideological, as practitioners and theorists began to question traditional values and design expressions. The work of the landscape architect Fletcher Steele, who incorporated aspects of what would become the modernist style into his plan for Naumkeag, Mabel Choate's estate in Stockbridge, Massachusetts, and early designs by Thomas Church, such as the Jerd Sullivan garden (1935) in San Francisco, exemplify this stylistic transition. The exhibition *Contemporary Landscape Architecture,* sponsored by the San Francisco Museum of Art in 1937, publicized recent work in the field, and Christopher Tunnard's pioneering book, *Gardens in the Modern Landscape* (1938), offered a "radical reconsideration of art, nature, and society as the basis for restructuring land-use practices for the entire environment."[10] These new ideas—and experiments in twentieth-century architecture, painting, and sculpture—inspired Dan Kiley, James Rose, and Garrett Eckbo to write a series of articles for *Pencil Points* that served as a catalyst for further change. It was an exciting time to be a design student.

At Berkeley, Royston was most influenced by Hollyngsworth Leland Vaughan, a former student of Thomas Church at Ohio State, who had become the youngest of the division's three faculty members in 1930. Known as a "young maverick," Vaughan taught his students—including Garrett Eckbo (class of '36)—"to keep an open mind and to form their own opinions."[11] In addition to his teaching, Vaughan worked in the Church office from 1931 to 1945 and in a professional partnership anchored by his partner and wife, Adele Wharton (class of '38). His design experiments in the new modes of form and spatial organization influenced by Cubism and Constructivism contrasted sharply with those of the program's two other full-time faculty, chair John Gregg and Harry Shepherd, both of whom advocated educating students in the Beaux-Arts tradition.[12] The classic codification of these design principles, Henry Hubbard and Theodora Kimball's *An Introduction to the Study of Landscape Design* (1917), was required reading in most American programs, but Vaughan cautioned against using the work of the past as an aesthetic smorgasbord of stylistic solutions. Instead, he presented history as a means of understanding the values embodied in landscape architecture—the first step in addressing the needs of twentieth-century American society. Royston vividly recalled Vaughan's approach to studio instruction: "He had a way of remaining silent, and it was his silence that taught me the most. He would come and look at my drawings and he just sort of grunted and that meant 'keep going' or if he started to talk about it then he'd just take you a little bit further on something. Usually if he said nothing he was approving."[13]

Along with Vaughan's Zen-like teaching, required courses in studio art influenced Royston. Reminiscing on his student days, he recalled learning "a great deal from my professors who were painters. . . . I learned about movement and about how things happen spatially in a painting. . . . I would look and look at a painting and then all of a sudden I could see the movement and the balance."[14] The three Berkeley professors Royston remembered as having the greatest impact on his education—the painters John Haley, Erle Loran, and Margaret Peterson—were prominent in the "Berkeley School," also known as the "Berkeley modernists." Under Haley's tutelage he learned basic design principles by creating abstract geometric compositions in black and white. Loran, an art historian who wrote a seminal text on Cézanne, taught him how to analyze the great paintings of Western tradition. Peterson, his drawing instructor, improved his drafting skills and critiqued his studio work in landscape architecture, providing a valuable interdisciplinary perspective. Royston's experiences with these accomplished American artists encouraged his growing conviction that landscape design flourishes in close dialogue with kindred arts.[15] Throughout his career, he would explore the relationship between painting and landscape architecture, challenging himself to improve his work by seeing "things in terms of structural dimension and movement," qualities he defined as the standards for success in both disciplines.[16] Perhaps most important, Royston found connections among all the arts—seeing three dimensions in a flat painting, artistry in structural engineering, and spatial excitement everywhere—and pushed himself to use his creativity to confront social issues.

Royston worked his way through college with odd jobs for the Division of Landscape Design and spent Saturdays in the Church office, which was quickly becoming one of the region's preeminent landscape architectural firms.[17] In the summer of 1937, a stint in the office of Arthur B. Hyde, a 1934 graduate of the Berkeley program, provided hands-on experience in the essentials of site work. The following summer Vaughan recommended Royston for a job in Church's office, where he joined the only other employee, Marie Harbeck. During this period, Royston recalled, Church "was working with all the modern architects at that time," including John Funk, Ernest Born, Gardner A. Dailey, Hervey Parke Clark, and William Wurster, among others.[18] He found himself well situated to become part of the regional network of design professionals.

As an apprentice, Royston contributed to several experimental projects that expanded his knowledge of modernist design. In 1939, he worked on Church's display gardens at the Golden Gate International Exposition in San Francisco. "Exhibition Garden A" employed a zigzag border fence and a concrete serpentine wall to divide areas of planting from redwood block paving. Thin pipe-stem columns supported the free-form roof of a small pavilion. Royston learned from his mentor's nonaxial design, bold juxtaposition of curvilinear and rectilinear geometries, and clear zoning of use areas.[19] He also benefited from working in the context of an exhibition in which international designers collaborated on modernist projects that stretched the limits of current practice. The exposition included "a dining room from Finland" with furniture by the modernist designers Alvar and Aino Aalto. About this time, Royston assisted the Russian-born architect Serge Chermayeff on an exhibit at Cargoes, a San Francisco store catering to the social elite (fig. 5). This job most likely came to him through Elizabeth Church, the first West Coast distributor of the fashionable modernist furniture by the Aaltos.[20]

During his final years at Berkeley, Royston began to develop his own design methodology. In addition to cultivating his interest in the biomorphic and Cubist forms of modern art, he studied the way Le Corbusier, Mies van der Rohe, and "the whole International School" designed using space rather than the more traditional, rigid geometry of the prevailing Beaux-Arts approach.[21] He came to believe that these new forms and spatial articulations, adapted to landscape architecture, would result in appropriate designs for contemporary America. Royston considered residential gardens designed as regurgitations of Medici villas absurd in the context of a democratic society, and park designs in the manner of the eighteenth-century English landscape

Fig. 5. Panel for Cargoes exhibit, c. 1940. Thomas D. Church Collection, EDA.

gardening tradition incapable of accommodating the recreational demands of twentieth-century citizens.[22] On his
own, he explored new aesthetic ideas by attending lectures
and exhibitions on modern art in the Bay Area. He was
especially drawn to the work of Kandinsky, with its charged
juxtapositions of sweeping arcs and converging diagonals.

He read the essays coauthored by Dan Kiley, James Rose, and Garrett Eckbo in *Architectural Record* and discovered he shared their desire for a new design perspective and methodology that would address the changing needs of twentieth-century society.[23]

Shortly after its founding in 1939, Royston joined Telesis, an informal group of designers and planners concerned with the environmental problems of the San Francisco region. Founded by architects, landscape architects, urban planners, and engineers, Telesis promoted rational, interdisciplinary regional planning. Members engaged in informal discussions, sponsoring workshops on such topics as housing and industrial design and advocating for the development of an indigenous "Bay Area style" emerging from the natural environment and its cultural history. Many of the region's most prominent academics and practitioners were members of the group, including William Wurster, Joseph Allen Stein, the architect Vernon DeMars, the landscape architect Geraldine Knight Scott, city planner T. J. Kent Jr., Eckbo, and Church.[24] It was through Telesis that Royston met Eckbo, with whom he quickly developed a friendship (fig. 6). In an introduction to an oral history on Eckbo, Royston described his memories of their times together before the war. "He loved to argue the cause of the common man, or the cause of design. We thoroughly enjoyed each other's company. Garrett liked jazz music as I did, and long evenings often were spent listening to the records of Kansas City, Chicago, New Orleans jazz and the blues. Lou Watters and his band were holding forth on Annie Street, behind the Palace Hotel, and there we frequently danced the night away. In those days we argued design, talked about new books, the state of the Union, politics and consumed vast quantities of red wine."[25]

As a senior, Royston lived in an apartment in Church's

Fig. 6. Royston and Garrett Eckbo in Canada, 1949. Photo by Evelyn Royston. RC EDA.

basement. In his little spare time, he participated in the university's drama club and summer stock performances with the Ross Players in Marin County. He later credited these experiences as an amateur actor with improving his ability to present his design work to large audiences.[26]

With Hitler's armies devastating Europe and Japan's imperialist forays in the Far East ever increasing, 1940 was a time of uncertainty, particularly for a young graduate of twenty-two launching a career. Fortunately, Royston's part-time work for Church led to a new opportunity—a coveted position in the renowned landscape architect's three-person office. In his private residential garden work, Church continued to experiment with new forms of expression, but he also expanded his practice to include larger-scale housing projects funded by the government. The office's frequent collaborations with prominent modernist Bay Area architects enhanced Royston's design education and contributed to his growing network of professional contacts.[27] Royston would fondly recall his apprenticeship with Church: "Our work consisted mostly of gardens, varying in size usually from one to five acres. It was a great training ground. . . . Those early years mark a special place in my memory. Tommy had a friendliness toward life in general, a way of enjoying his profession that fostered an office ambiance conducive to creativity. His design was quiet and sure, a transitionist in detail and space, Victorian and yet modern."[28]

Soon after Royston began work with Church, the office obtained several significant commissions for large-scale housing projects, including Park Merced (1941–1950), a two-hundred-acre housing project on the western edge of San Francisco, for the Metropolitan Insurance Company. Church and the architect Leonard Schultze collaborated on "the basic architectural concept, the pie-shaped blocks," while Royston served as project landscape architect.[29] Working with Douglas Baylis and his UC Berkeley mentor Leland Vaughan, Royston produced designs for the housing block's many inner courtyards and saw the first phase of the project through to completion. Park Merced's clear separation of automobile and pedestrian circulation influenced the site-planning principles Royston would apply throughout his practice, especially in suburban parks, college campuses, and new towns.[30] The success of the plan led to the firm's involvement in permanent low-income housing in San Francisco, including Potrero Terrace, where Royston was in charge of supervising the installation of the planting plan, a difficult task that required a crew of twenty using jackhammers to drill planting holes in the site's solid bedrock. Royston also worked on the landscape design of Valencia Gardens public housing, designed by William Wurster, and supervised its on-site completion, which included sculptures by Beniamino Bufano sponsored by the Federal Art Project (fig. 7).[31] In addition, Royston recalled completing "at least twenty major temporary housing projects in the Bay Area" before he left for the navy, noting almost thirty-five years later that "the houses are all gone, but the trees are there."[32]

The entry of the United States in the Second World War interrupted Royston's promising career, and suddenly the "war became quite personal." Church had written letters to defer his draft status because of the firm's involvement with war housing projects, but one evening Royston and Eckbo decided to join a naval officer training program.[33] Although Eckbo was rejected for medical reasons, Royston enlisted and was quickly deployed in the South Pacific. "I wanted

Fig. 7. Valencia Gardens, San Francisco, n.d. RC EDA.

to go. I wanted to stop Hitler. . . . They were days of terror really. You just couldn't understand what was going on. . . . It was a horrible experience to be with the dead and the fact that you [the U.S. forces] had done it. . . . It is what you see, hear, smell and touch in death that turns the mind and I was no exception. I can still remember those kinds of things. . . . you grew up fast."[34]

At first Royston ferried marines to the beaches under fire. On being promoted to first lieutenant, he was charged with loading and repairing the USS *Pondera,* his attack transport. In the rare quiet moments his demanding duties allowed, he sketched and modeled imaginary residences and gardens, ideal visions of space and form he hoped to create when peace returned. He also fashioned playful pieces of jewelry for his wife Evelyn, whom he had married in 1941.[35] More than mere diversions, these design exercises were continuing explorations of new ideas. Royston credited them with his development of more complex spatial organizations in his postwar work.[36]

Near the end of his deployment Royston accepted— through correspondence—the offer of a partnership that included Eckbo and his brother-in-law, Edward Williams (fig. 8).[37] Because of his admiration for Church, this was not an easy decision, but Royston felt drawn by the challenge of a situation where "we could experiment right and left."[38] After logging 150,000 miles at sea, he returned to San Francisco in 1946 to join the new firm. He recalled, "When I sailed through the Golden Gate I wasn't going anywhere ever again. Ever! I mean it took me fifteen years to make a major trip."[39]

As Royston soon discovered, the war had transformed the Bay Area. Thousands of returning servicemen arrived at the ports of Oakland and San Francisco and chose to remain in the region. This boom in growth was nourished by post-

Fig. 8. The principals of Eckbo, Royston & Williams: (*left to right*) Garrett Eckbo, Francis Dean, Edward Williams, and Robert Royston, 1949. RC EDA.

war industrial expansion, high-paying jobs, and an acute housing shortage, as well as generous support of home mortgages by the Federal Housing Authority and the GI Bill. Booster rhetoric sustained the alluring myth of California as a paradise blessed with a mild climate, beautiful unspoiled landscape, and abundant economic opportunity; Hollywood films, orange crate labels, and popular magazines like *Sunset* and *House Beautiful* drew people from across the nation to venture into new beginnings. The resulting growth rate was astonishing.[40] From 1940 to 1950 the urban population of California grew by nearly 50 percent, the greatest increase in the nation. The most volatile growth occurred on the edges of existing towns and cities, creating the suburbs where Royston would find most of his clients.[41]

When Royston returned to the Bay Area and walked into his new firm's San Francisco office, he found his partners working on an innovative housing project. In 1945, Eckbo, Royston & Williams had received the commission to design Ladera, a 258-acre cooperative housing development near Palo Alto. The Peninsula Housing Association, the private group that hired the firm, hoped to create a more democratic, affordable alternative to the rapidly growing Bay Area suburbs. In a joint effort with a team of architects and engineers characteristic of what Royston later called "the spirit of collaboration and the unusually free interchange of ideas" among professionals in the Bay Area, Royston and Eckbo created a linear park linking residential clusters, school, church, and commercial facilities. Their plan also separated pedestrian circulation from automobile traffic.[42] Although Ladera had proved an economic failure by 1949, the project provided the new firm with crucial experience in cooperative work and would become a precedent for Royston's fundamental conceptual framework—the "landscape matrix," an interconnected system of various types of open spaces—that he would develop over the course of his long career.

After just two years, Eckbo moved to Los Angeles to establish the firm's second office. The San Francisco office continued to operate independently, with Royston doing most of the design work and Williams managing the business affairs. The partners met once a month in the small town of Paso Robles, halfway between the two cities, to exchange ideas, discuss the status of current projects, and engage in a lively critique of each other's work, in keeping with their belief in the value of collaboration.[43] In 1948, the landscape architect Francis Dean joined the firm.

At this point about 80 percent of the new firm's commissions were residential gardens, which Royston considered "fun projects" that allowed him to develop relationships with clients who were willing to experiment with new ideas. During this period he produced some of his most outstanding designs: the Naify garden in Atherton (1947), the garden for his own home and that of his neighbor, the architect Joseph Allen Stein, in Mill Valley (1947), and the Wilson garden (1948), also in Mill Valley. In several of these, he devised innovative solutions to the challenges of difficult sites. For the Naifys, he created a new entry sequence, regrading and framing the site with a bold arc of trees (see fig. 2). For his own backyard he designed a courtyard on a steep gradient, later expanding it to include a projecting deck with a view of Mount Tamalpais, a major landmark of the Bay Area (fig. 9). His design for the Wilson garden involved screening an unsightly view with a forty-foot-long, six-foot-high hori-

Fig. 9. Deck addition to the Royston garden, c. 1970. RC EDA.

Fig. 10. Model of the Wilson garden with "sky plane" trellis, 1949. JCM.

zontal trellis he called a "sky plane" (fig. 10). The second Appert garden, in Atherton (1950), with Joseph Stein as the architect, was structured around an elaborate multilevel terrace. Featured in such publications as *Sunset, House & Garden, Arts & Architecture, Architectural Record,* and *House Beautiful,* these commissions helped establish Royston's reputation as a gifted young designer.[44]

In this early residential work, Royston developed the sensitive, client-oriented approach to design which characterized his career. After interviewing a client and visiting the site, he produced a scaled plan based on a topographical survey of the property. Next he drew a garden diagram showing areas of use arranged to avoid functional conflicts such as placing a quiet space for contemplation next to a children's play area. Royston used the diagram to inform his final design, considering alternatives as he worked, but always delivering a single finished plan. Presentation drawings often included isometric plans highlighting the spatial qualities of the design and perspective sketches to help clients visualize their gardens. For clients who enjoyed gardening, Royston located the planting beds without specifying individual species.[45]

While codirecting the San Francisco office and developing his personal approach to design, Royston also ventured into a full-time academic career. In 1947, he began teaching at his alma mater in the Division of Landscape Design, where he shared his professional experiences with his students, many of whom were degree candidates in architecture. He recruited two of the most gifted, Asa Hanamoto and David R. Mayes, to work in the San Francisco office. As the new partnership established itself, Royston's academic salary helped to keep the firm solvent and support his growing family. His first child, Michel Ann Royston, was born in 1947.[46]

Royston consistently strove to create positive psychological experiences through his design work, and as a teacher at UC Berkeley (and later at Stanford) he taught his students to do so as well. During these years he read *The Language of Vision* (1944), a groundbreaking book on cognition and design by the Hungarian-born artist and theorist Gyorgy Kepes. The book "made so much sense" to Royston, who agreed with Kepes's understanding of how the artistic manipulation of color, space, and texture influenced human perception.[47] *The Language of Vision* was most likely the catalyst for Royston's development of "the model box," a device he created to help his students analyze the psychological effects of the spaces they designed. This simple forty-eight-inch-square wooden box, eighteen inches high, had a translucent top allowing light to enter and was mounted on a revolving stand at eye level. Students placed scale models of their

Fig. 11. Student study models in Royston's "model box," n.d. JCM.

Fig. 12. Paving patterns study model, n.d. JCM.

work in the box and studied them through a viewing hole (fig. 11). Royston also created abstract study models with interchangeable parts, such as vertical planes with different degrees of transparency and paving patterns of varying texture and visual complexity (fig. 12). He gathered his students around the model box and manipulated this assortment of parts to change degrees of transparency, expand and contract spaces, and alter the composition of solids and voids. As he moved elements within the box, he asked his students questions such as, "If you increased the width of this space and reduced its degree of enclosure, how would you feel if you occupied it?"[48]

In 1948, the department's student publication, *Axis,* changed its name to *Space,* heralding a new era in design at Berkeley. The next year, the program was restructured as a full-fledged Department of Landscape Architecture, chaired by Royston's mentor Leland Vaughan. Along with his colleagues, Vaughan revised the curriculum to focus on modernist design. The department attracted full-time faculty sympathetic to innovation, including R. B. Litton Jr., Francis Violich, Mai Arbegast, and Robert Tetlow, and welcomed young visiting practitioners who were experimenting with new ideas about space and materials, such as Theodore Osmundson, Lawrence Halprin, Douglas Baylis, and Geraldine Knight Scott. A dynamic, closely bound community of professionals and academics began to develop, and from this crucible of design theory would emerge two of the era's most important books on landscape architecture: Garrett Eckbo's *Landscape for Living* (1950) and Thomas Church's *Gardens Are for People* (1955).[49] Royston's professional experience, prowess as a teacher, and design talent placed him at the forefront of this innovative design community (fig. 13).[50]

As a young professor at one of the country's most progressive design schools, Royston joined in the quest for new design methods but also discovered a passion for the literature

Fig. 13. Royston critiquing student work at UC Berkeley, 1949. RC EDA.

of social science and urban planning. One of the most influential works shaping his thought during his first years of teaching at Berkeley was *Planning the Neighborhood,* a ninety-page government publication sponsored by the American Public Health Association Committee on the Hygiene of Housing.[51] Royston assigned it as required reading in his Berkeley studios. *Planning the Neighborhood* had the ring of a manifesto and was aimed at addressing the "crisis" of the national housing shortage in the immediate postwar period, but its ideas dated back to Clarence Perry's writings of the late 1920s. Royston was especially attracted to Perry and N. L. Engelhardt's notion of the "neighborhood" as a building block of urban planning, and he passed their ideas on to his students.[52] He advocated for the development of neighborhoods of about six thousand people, a size that would allow most children to live within a quarter mile of their elementary school. In addition to its educational function, the neighborhood school would serve as a center for meetings and social activities and include a park serving all local residents. Royston knew that single-family detached houses were preferred, but also envisioned high-rise apartments and townhouses in his ideal neighborhood. Although some critics viewed suburbs divided into neighborhood units as breeding grounds for dysfunctional lifestyles, Royston believed that enlightened site planning could encourage shared community values, a concept he expressed in his teachings and practice.[53]

During this early phase of his career, Royston ventured into park design—a project type then considered "one of the dullest things you could do—a few trees and a baseball field."[54] Unlike his colleagues, who considered such commissions pedestrian, Royston found himself inspired by the idea of park design and enthusiastically took on the firm's commission for the Rod & Gun Club in Point Richmond

on the north shore of San Francisco Bay. The park he created for Standard Oil Refinery employees and their families
in 1950 rejected the prevalent notion of parks as outdoor
gymnasiums primarily catering to children and young adults
while neglecting the elderly. His new vision included numerous family picnic areas, barbecue pits, swimming pools, and
separate play areas for children of different ages. The park's
windbreaks and pergolas were reminiscent of private garden
amenities. These details created a feeling of familiarity and
intimacy, as if the entire park were a residential garden with
specialized equipment for play and for entertaining.[55]

Concurrent with the completion of the Standard Oil
employee park, Royston and his colleagues began work on
St. Mary's Square in San Francisco's Chinatown district (fig.
14). It was Royston's first major commission in a dense urban

Fig. 14. St. Mary's Square, 2017. JCM.

area. This rooftop plaza and green over a new parking structure provided much-needed public open space to the most densely populated neighborhood of the city. Royston collaborated with the garage's designers to integrate its structural system with the design of the rooftop square. The garage was partially operative by 1954, and the square was completed three years later as the final phase of construction.

His design for the Chinn garden (1951) in a small area behind a four-story apartment building was also located in San Francisco's Chinatown, a short walk from St. Mary's Square. This remarkable garden illustrates how his work began to blur the boundaries between the artistic and the utilitarian, as well as between public and private space. As seen from the fourth floor, where his clients lived, the garden suggested a Mondrian painting; on the ground level, it offered a colorful, low-maintenance space for the residents to enjoy (fig. 15).[56] Royston's interest in schools, neighborhoods, and community life had become more personal as his own family continued to grow; his son Curtis Robert Royston was born in 1951.

The paranoia of the McCarthy era ended Royston's full-time position as an academic. He refused to sign the loyalty oath demanded of all its employees by the state of California and was forced to resign his assistant professorship. A fervent advocate of freedom of thought, he leaned to the left politically but was not a radical. Throughout his life he remained a Democrat, with a firm belief in the potential of government to promote social justice and intelligent environmental stewardship. Shortly after resigning from Berkeley in 1951, he became a visiting professor at North Carolina State University.[57] He would also teach courses in "visual perception" and urban design in the architecture department at Stanford in 1956 and ultimately serve as a guest critic or lecturer

Fig. 15. Chinn garden, 1951. Photo by Ernest Braun, Ernest Braun Archives (EBA).

in departments of architecture or landscape architecture in twenty-four universities. This long association with academia helped Royston maintain a critical perspective on his own work through dialogue with colleagues and students.

At Berkeley, Royston had designed the landscape for Dwinelle Hall in 1950 and, despite his resignation, would acquire commissions for the Home Economics Building (1953) and the School of Public Health (1954), among other projects. Over the next decade, as the campus expanded to embrace technology, Royston's firm was commissioned to create a master plan for the university's top-secret Lawrence Livermore National Laboratory (1968), as well as more detailed plans for several buildings on the Livermore campus.[58]

After leaving his academic position, Royston further developed the design concepts crystallized in *Planning the Neighborhood,* many of which he had put into practice in the Ladera cooperative housing project. His ideas were informed by the literature of urban planning, especially the works of H. W. S. Cleveland, Lewis Mumford, Clarence Perry, John Nolen, Ebenezer Howard, and the Olmsted firm. The innovative site plans for Radburn, New Jersey, and Greenbelt, Maryland, also influenced his development of the "landscape matrix," a flexible network of open spaces—parks, plazas, parkways, and nature preserves—adapted to the local topography, drainage systems, climate, soil, and cultural context.[59] The matrix established a "strong framework" by "the linking of open space as a continuous system throughout the community."[60] Royston's modernist vision incorporated both the interconnected spaces of Olmsted and Vaux's work, as exemplified by their plan for Buffalo, New York, and the "continuous open space" championed in *Planning the Neighborhood* as a structural element of a city.

Within the landscape matrix, Royston included a variety of park types in accord with the *Guide for Planning Recreation Parks in California* (1956), which influenced the planning commissions and park departments he collaborated with throughout the state.[61] The publication offered detailed descriptions of facilities and acreage recommendations for a hierarchy of parks ranging from neighborhood playlots to large city parks of fifty acres or more. Royston readily accepted the size specifications but supplemented the recommended facilities with ideas of his own. He envisioned his park and plaza designs within a postwar city composed of a central business district linked to suburbs through public rail transportation or the region's rapidly emerging multilane automobile freeway systems. In his professional practice, he hoped to bring order to this pattern of unchecked urban growth, with its disastrous consequences for the quality of human life and natural ecosystems. Royston took a practical approach to design but also declared his parks "a new art form."[62] He began to develop a more comprehensive view of park design that not only considered each site as part of a larger planned system or matrix but also addressed the character of individual parks and their users in new, creative ways. In the 1960s, he would use the matrix idea as the basis for the interconnected green spaces of his college campus plans.

During the fifties, Royston explored new concepts in his designs of playgrounds, rethinking the nature of how children play a decade before the architects M. Paul Friedberg and Richard Dattner created the first "adventure playgrounds" in New York City. Throughout Europe and the United States this was a time of innovation in playground design, with pioneering work by Aldo van Eyck in Holland, Alfred Trachsel and Alfred Ledermann in Switzerland, and Marjory Allen in the United Kingdom. Playgrounds were regarded as important commissions by architectural and landscape architectural firms and featured in professional journals such as *Architectural Record*. In 1954, the toy company Creative Playthings, *Parents' Magazine,* and the Museum of Modern Art in New York cosponsored a play sculpture competition featuring abstract design meant to encourage imagination and creativity, similar to the types of three-dimensional forms Royston incorporated in his park playgrounds.

While he was aware of the work of his peers, Royston preferred to rely on his own creativity.[63] For inspiration, he drew on childhood memories, observed his own children, and studied how playgrounds were used. He instilled a sense of adventure in his designs for Krusi Park in Alameda (1954), Pixie Place in Ross (1954), and his subsequent public parks by developing play equipment to stimulate the imagination (fig. 16). Royston's innovations contrast with public parks characteristic of his day, which lacked variety in programmatic elements and offered limited, standardized equipment—typically swings, slides, seesaws, and climbing bars ordered from catalogs. He worked from the blueprint outlined in *Planning the Neighborhood* and the guidelines in that document for the "Community Recreation Park" to create new, sculptural

Fig. 16. Pixie Place, n.d. Photo by Royston. JCM.

settings for children's play, as well as for the enjoyment of adults. Mitchell Park, for example, included an area for small children within a larger twenty-acre park, with "freeform shapes that evoke the biomorphic sculpture of European artists such as Jean Arp" (fig. 17).[64] All playground equipment, seating, and lighting were custom designed, unique to each site, and considered works of art. Construction on Mitchell Park, Royston's tour de force, began in 1955, the year his third child, Tonia Lee Royston, was born.

Mitchell Park combined the functional zoning, layered spaces, and residential-scale details of the Rod & Gun Club

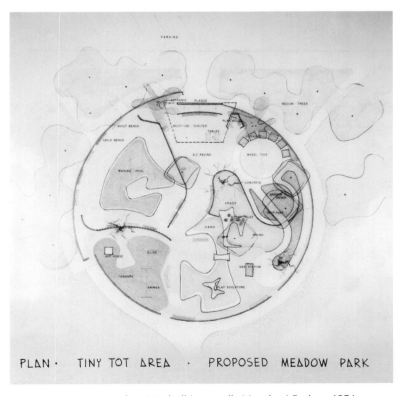

Fig. 17. Tiny Tot Area plan, Mitchell (originally Meadow) Park, c. 1956. RC EDA.

Fig. 18. Mitchell Park multi-use slab, 2014. Office of Reed Dillingham.

with the fresh playground design and abstract play structures of Krusi Park. Royston's innovations included a sculpted ground plane forming a series of space-defining berms, a richer planting design palette, a perimeter treatment with views into the center of the park, more facilities for the elderly, and new types of multipurpose play equipment. The park attracted national attention and was toured by Greek, Egyptian, and Japanese delegates to the 1958 International Recreation Congress.[65] One of the clearest embodiments of Royston's concept of a park as a public garden, Mitchell Park was also one of the most precedent-setting public spaces of its kind (fig. 18).

In 1958, Royston, seeking greater independence, departed from Eckbo and Williams. He formed his own firm— Royston, Hanamoto & Mayes (RHM)—with David Mayes and Asa Hanamoto, his former students and coworkers at ERW. The late 1950s were a time of marked transition for many landscape architectural firms nationwide. A flourishing economy grounded in federal and state government initiatives, as well as private corporate expansion, resulted in a wide range of project types, such as office parks, large-scale land use plans, new towns, and shopping centers. Private garden commissions, the lifeblood of most offices in the 1940s and early 1950s, became less desirable as larger-scale, more lucrative commissions beckoned. These new opportunities demanded decisive changes in office structure. As firms expanded, the old studio system was replaced by a new corporate organization, and project managers coordinating larger teams of specialists became the norm. Many firms originally composed almost exclusively of landscape architects began to hire their own in-house specialists, such as architects, planners, and structural and civil engineers. After Royston left, Eckbo and Williams founded EDAW (with Francis Dean and Don Austin) along corporate lines. Among the many firms making a similar transition were SWA (Hideo Sasaki, Peter Walker, and Associates), POD (Process Oriented Design), JJR (Carl Johnson, Bill Johnson, and Clarence Roy), and HOK (George Hellmuth, Gyo Obata, and George Kassabaum). Thomas Church successfully continued his smaller studio practice, although he occasionally referred projects beyond his scope to Royston's firm.

In his new San Francisco firm, restructured to resemble the corporate model, Royston continued relationships with earlier clients but also took on a variety of new projects, including consultation on master plans for the University of Utah in Salt Lake City and the Stanford Linear Accelerator Center (1961) in Menlo Park. RHM acquired significant landscape and planning commissions in the cities of Fremont, Hayward, Palo Alto, and Mountain View, among other rapidly growing Bay Area communities. The landscape architect Patricia A. Carlisle and the architect Louis G. Alley joined the firm at this time.[66]

Building on his earlier work at the Rod & Gun Club and Mitchell Park, Royston designed a series of sophisticated new parks tailored to the needs of their users. At Palo Alto's Bowden Park (1960), a three-acre park across from a commuter rail station, he envisioned the experiences of daily commuters and included spaces for children's play, eating areas, and quiet meeting places. Additional opportunities for Royston to synthesize his park planning ideas came through commissions for Santa Clara's Central Park (1960–1975) and the Santa Clara Civic Center Park (1963–1964). Like all of his park designs, the plan for Central Park carefully considered the user's experience of space and how this might change over time. Circuit walks offered a rich sequence of open meadows and shaded groves to explore. Plants were used to create visual barriers and focus attention on elements of interest. Paths led to surprises—a glistening fountain in a lake or a large mound of wildflowers—that varied according to season. Royston conceived of plants as sculpture, but also emphasized them "as building space. . . . When you get into plant materials they are the walls. I realized they are growing walls. . . . As your material grows it is kind of wonderful to contemplate" (fig. 19).[67]

While Royston's theory of the psychological effects of space was central to his work, he almost entirely avoided the use of iconography to enrich such spatial experience. At the same time, he willingly adjusted his principles to meet public expectations. When citizens of Santa Clara wanted a popular sculptor's statue of the city's namesake, St. Clare, in the middle of Santa Clara Civic Center Park, he complied. Royston was most interested in the immediate experience of space and consciously manipulated it to evoke desirable states of mind, such as a sense of security, peace, exhilaration, or curiosity. His main goal was to create "spaces that move far beyond the practical into the delightful."[68]

Fig. 19. Central Park chain arbor with vines, 2005. Photo by Reuben Rainey.

In 1960, as he was developing his concept for the American public park, Royston gained a client who would both open the door to numerous commissions and offer a new window into the realities of suburban life. Edward P. Eichler, son of the prescient real estate developer Joseph L. Eichler, hired Royston's office to collaborate with the architecture firm Anshen & Allen on a garden for his new home in Atherton. The success of this initial project led to multiple commissions from the senior Eichler's firm, Eichler Homes, Inc., between 1960 and 1966. Eichler emphasized progressive modernist design and worked closely with teams of architects, landscape architects, and interior designers, in many cases developing lasting friendships. Royston's affable nature was well suited to Eichler's approach, which resembled that of his own office, and he worked with each of Eichler's architects: Anshen & Allen, Jones & Emmons, and later Claude Oakland.[69]

These collaborations resulted in dozens of built projects, including landscapes for apartment developments, gardens for model homes and sales offices in various Eichler residential subdivisions, the landscape setting and patios for the Eichler Homes office headquarters in Palo Alto, and a master plan for the Lucas Valley planned community (1962) in Marin County. The Lucas Valley plan was reminiscent of Royston's earlier work at Ladera in that it included a school and a shopping center, but the smaller site and limited development budget precluded the separate pedestrian path system found in the earlier plan (fig. 20). Royston also collaborated with Eichler and the firm Anshen & Allen on Stanford University's Jordan Quad, a complex of classrooms, student residences, and faculty offices.[70] Beyond the direct work for the developer, the demonstration gardens created for the model homes brought numerous new homeowners to the Royston office looking for gardens suited to their innovative homes.

An increasing number of specialized commissions, as well as the area's growing reputation as a center of innova-

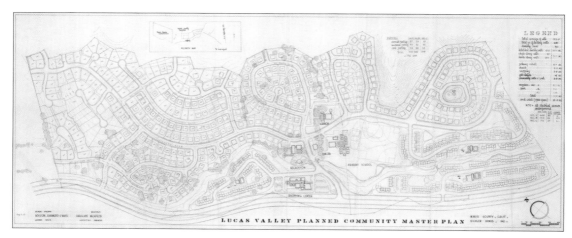

Fig. 20. Lucas Valley, Marin County, master plan, 1965. RC EDA.

tion and technology, led Royston to expand his firm in 1960, with the promotion of Eldon Beck from associate to fourth principal.[71] This would be the first of three major expansions in his partnership, a change typical of the times as landscape architecture firms scrambled to meet the demands of the generation. In addition to the Eichler projects and some of the earliest landscapes for corporations in what would become known as Silicon Valley, the expanded firm grappled with more traditional urban project types—parks, urban spaces, and subsidized housing.

Over the next decade, Royston returned to public housing design, taking on commissions from the San Francisco Redevelopment Agency for master landscape plans of the Hunter's Point (1962) and Western Addition (1965) projects, and, in 1967, serving on the Housing and Urban Development Region VI Advisory Committee. His work for the Redevelopment Agency included collaborating with the architect Clement Chen Jr. on the Chinese Cultural and Trade Center (Portsmouth Square Park). One of his major commissions in the private sector came from the Bethel African Methodist Episcopal Church, which hired him to create landscape designs for Freedom West, a "transitional housing community" in San Francisco.[72] In all of his designs, Royston considered the psychological, social, and recreational needs of those most likely to share his spaces.

The commissions entering the Royston office throughout the 1960s are notable for their variety, which reflected not only the times but also Royston's willingness to acquire highly specialized projects. This work included public infrastructure such as bridges and water treatment plants. Beginning in the late 1950s, the office worked with the East Bay Municipal Utilities District on multiple projects, including the cover for the Estates Reservoir in Piedmont, California, which was completed in 1968. With the exception of the Chinn garden in San Francisco, the design of the Estates Reservoir is Royston's most explicit expression of landscape as abstract art. During this time, Royston's firm also designed corporate landscapes for Hewlett Packard in Palo Alto and Raychem in Menlo Park, among other new technological research corporations, as well as for the developers Renault & Handley, who offered them over twenty commercial commissions in the Bay Area. In addition, RHMB developed landscapes for Bay Area Rapid Transit (BART), the new public transportation system linking the region's metropolitan areas, and a linear park for the city of Albany in 1965 (figs. 21, 22).

When David Mayes left the firm in 1966 to launch his own practice, Kazuo Abey became the new fourth partner.

Fig. 21. BART station entry plaza sketch, 1966. RC EDA.

Fig. 22. Albany, CA, linear park under BART line, 1965. RC EDA.

Another Berkeley graduate, Harold Kobayashi, also played a prominent role in the reorganized firm, which consisted of six principals, four associates, and a staff of fifteen. RHBA included specialists in regional and urban planning, engineering, architecture, forestry, and business management (fig. 23). The following year the firm designed a plan for Ashby Place Station, which eventually became part of the overall transit corridor design for the East Bay section of BART.

Also in 1967, Thomas Church brought two commissions to RHBA with the understanding that he would collaborate as a consultant: the design for the Upper Quarry Amphitheater at UC Santa Cruz and a master plan for Thacher School in Ojai. The Santa Cruz campus had special meaning for Church, the landscape architect of the university's original long-range development plan in the early 1960s, and

Fig. 23. Royston, Hanamoto, Beck & Abey staff, c. 1969. JCM.

he offered unique insight into the native landscape and its features. For the amphitheater, RHBA and Church incorporated rock from a nineteenth-century quarry on the site and created a series of asymmetrical terraces with angled benches in an effort to mirror the surrounding rock outcroppings, one of which pierced through the stage (fig. 24). A stand of bigleaf maple served as a backdrop. The Quarry Amphitheater, now the center of an impressive restoration effort, won an AIA merit award in 1968.[73] The Thacher School was founded on the ideal of nature as a classroom, and the RHBA plan emphasized the local hills, mountains, native oak, and chaparral of the Ojai Valley. The commission may have come to Church through local connections, as he lived in Ojai as a child.

During this decade, RHBA also took on landscapes for regional colleges, including the master plan for the fifteenth

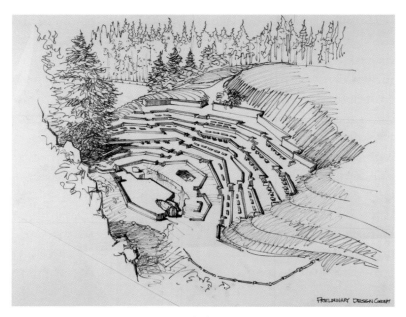

Fig. 24. UC Santa Cruz Quarry Amphitheater, sketch, 1966. RC EDA.

university in the California state system, Stanislaus College in the Central Valley; a design for UC San Francisco Medical Center that included a trail system and roof deck, a central campus court, and even campus furniture; and the landscape of Merrill College and the student center at Cowell College, among other work for UC Santa Cruz. Even as the firm continued to expand and its projects multiplied, Royston never lost sight of one of his fundamental ideals— the landscape matrix. At De Anza Community College (c. 1966) in Cupertino and San Joaquin Delta College (1969–1978) in Stockton, Royston would apply this concept to planning a college campus. For the site plan at San Joaquin Delta, RHBA, with principal Eldon Beck serving as head designer, located student commuter parking on the perimeter of the site and a pedestrian complex of buildings in the center. Wide walkways densely planted with trees connected the perimeter parking lots with the central campus. The academic buildings were elevated on earthen berms, making them visible as civic landmarks within the surrounding community of Stockton. A central plaza, shaded by a heavy tree canopy that wrapped around the bordering buildings, provided outdoor classrooms and meeting spaces. The planting plan specified hardy, low-maintenance vegetation, an indication of the firm's growing concern with environmental issues. The same skillful integration of architecture and landscape was achieved at De Anza College, where buildings were elevated on berms to increase their visibility and small plazas served as outdoor classrooms in a pedestrian precinct. Coast live oak and other native plants were preserved and banks of grass left unmowed.[74]

In 1968, RHBA was also hired to design a long-range development plan for the Lawrence Radiation Laboratory (renamed the Lawrence Livermore Laboratory in 1972) about a half hour southeast of UC Berkeley, its parent institution. The site had previously accommodated a naval air station, laid out on a grid, and new development was crowded into a corner of the site. Royston's concept for a more flexible campus, with a curvilinear layout, evolved from the type of basic question he liked to pose: "Should a great laboratory continue to be controlled by a road system and flying field adapted for training aviators in World War II?" By shifting the planning scheme from a grid to a less formal pattern and laying out a loop road system, he created spaces for new development, improved access to buildings, and provided areas for planting trees. The "Royston Plan," as it became known, "produced a campus-like setting" and "was so visionary that it retains its integrity after more than forty years."[75]

While designing his plan for the self-contained, high-security facility, Royston also found an opportunity to experiment with his landscape matrix ideal at two sites free of preexisting structures—Sunriver, Oregon, and North Bonneville, Washington. He designed the private recreational community of Sunriver on a 5,500-acre tract at the base of the Cascade Range in 1969. The housing was designed as a cluster of "villages" within a hierarchy of linked parks and recreational trails. When North Bonneville, a hamlet founded in the 1930s, was moved to a new site after the construction of a second powerhouse next to Bonneville Dam, Royston designed its new town plan. The landscape contractor Harold Watkin described the job, which involved handling "something like eight or nine million yards of rock or fill . . . and still use it so it doesn't look like a big rock pile."[76] Royston's matrix is a continuous green space linking the small town center with a park and elementary school. A system of pedestrian paths extends from this central area to residential cul-de-sacs.

In the midst of these experiments, RHBA landed the commission to create a plan for the ski town of Vail, Colorado, an urban planning challenge that borrowed many principles from the matrix concept. Royston presented the preliminary plan at a Vail trustees' meeting in 1973. RHBA's "Vail Plan," which focused on creating a pedestrian-friendly village core, included a transportation terminal and plaza, pedestrian walks, malls and plazas, a new town entrance, a community aquatic center, and areas dedicated to open space. The transportation terminal won a U.S. Department of Transportation honor award in "The Highway and Its Environment" category in 1977. Eldon Beck, a lifelong skier, was lead designer on the project.

During the 1970s, RHBA became more intensely involved in environmental issues through its work on detailed planning and assessment reports for the Golden Gate

National Recreation Area (GGNRA), at more than eighty thousand acres one of the largest urban parks in the world (fig. 25). The firm's studies of Muir Woods, Fort Point, and Point Reyes, along with its structural safety hazard study for Alcatraz, helped shape the National Park Service's policies for natural and cultural landscapes.[77] RHBA's work for GGNRA demonstrated the firm's commitment to the regional environment—the largest and perhaps most crucial element of the landscape matrix—and laid the foundation for the firm's future large-scale park work; in 2016, RHAA was involved in almost fifty projects in ten national parks.[78]

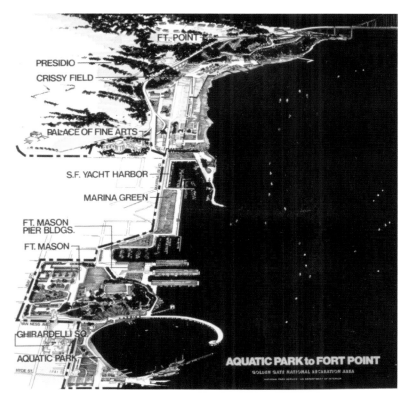

Fig. 25. Golden Gate National Recreation Area, plan, c. 1975. EDA.

Following RHBA's success at Vail, Eldon Beck left in 1979 to focus on ski resort design, and Louis Alley took his place in the partnership.[79] The firm of Royston, Hanamoto, Alley & Abey (RHAA) offered "environmental planning and analysis," "community planning," "urban planning and design," and "land and water reclamation and restoration," as well as standard professional services. Its mission statement asserted a far-ranging, humanistic approach to design, an effort "to conserve, to build, and to shape the landscape for people to use and enjoy" and focus on "the quality of the landscape . . . whether it be large or small, urban or rural, tamed or wild."[80] Royston fully embraced collaboration as the necessary means of completing the increasingly complex projects taken on by the firm. These included master plans for the Los Alamos National Laboratory (1980) and RHAA's first major international project, Parque del Recuerdo cemetery in Santiago, Chile (1981).[81]

The firm received the Chilean commission based on its design for Riverside National Cemetery, a project that set the standard for Veterans Administration cemeteries throughout the country (fig. 26). For the Parque del Recuerdo plan, RHAA produced a bold, highly geometrical radial design featuring two large burial areas of concentric circles connected by multiple drives (fig. 27). This commission led to other international opportunities, including contracts for flood control projects in Japan and Taiwan, the National Heroes Cemetery and Taman Kiara National Arboretum in Kuala Lumpur, Jurong Bird Park in Singapore, and Kaohsiung Metropolitan Park and Yangmingshan National Park in Taiwan. In 1986, Royston described RHAA's approach to such international commissions: "We spend time at the drawing boards in the respective countries. We have opened offices or shared office space in Malaysia and in Singapore.

Fig. 26. Riverside National Cemetery, Riverside, CA, 2016. Photo by JC Miller.

Fig. 27. Parque del Recuerdo, Santiago, Chile, c. 1995. RHAA.

This time spent abroad by our team . . . is invaluable as it gives us a chance to work with the site on a day-to-day basis and to collaborate closely with the client and our local consultants, listening to and learning from them about their work and the symbols of their country."[82]

Because the firm worked as a team, especially on these later international commissions, the extent of Royston's individual contribution is impossible to discern, but he "signed off on every drawing leaving the office" and remained the firm's chief presenter of its major projects to clients.[83] His experience as an amateur actor served him well. His resonant voice, self-confidence, contagious optimism, and sturdy six-foot frame gave him a powerful stage presence in front of town meetings, planning commissions, and corporate boards. As the leader of the firm, Royston excelled not only in selling its services but also in explaining projects in broad contextual terms—as significant contributions to the postwar American city. Royston's successful transition from a small office to a pioneering corporate firm is also a testament to his management style. He supervised hiring and promotions and created a harmonious workplace by listening to employees' suggestions and fostering each individual's professional development through personal attention.[84]

In 1980, Evelyn Dunwoody Royston, his spouse of thirty-nine years, died after a long illness. Two years later, Royston married Hannelore Gothe, and they raised her two young daughters, Danielle Machotka and Julia Anne Machotka, in Mill Valley. Near the end of his career, in March 1986, Royston was invited by the Design Arts Board of Australia to chair the jury for the nation's first "National Projects Awards in Landscape Architecture." Before his visit, the editors of *Landscape Australia* magazine invited him to write two articles—the clearest printed statements of his design methodology. "A Brief History," published in the fall of 1986, summarized his professional practice, before shifting to an optimistic reflection on the future of the profession. He welcomed the increasing number of projects using computer data analysis to study environmental issues, while reaffirming the value of landscape architecture as "a fine art" requiring a strong aesthetic sensibility. After noting the many accomplishments of landscape architects in protecting the natural environment and enhancing the quality of human life, he concluded, "We will build upon the past, and the magnitude of our contribution to society will grow."[85]

The second article, "Robert Royston's Thoughts on Landscape Architecture," comprises forty-one brief comments distilled from his experience in the field. He covers a range of subjects: the need for well-planned cities formed around a matrix of parks, the importance of team design, the necessity for citizen input in the design process, the challenge of playground design, the importance of intuition, and the danger of strict design guidelines that stifle creativity, among others. He concludes with thoughts directed "to all who remain students":

> The substance of design is found by study,
> by the observation of nature,
> by analysis of form and function in history, past and present,
> by the successes and errors of human decision, as people shape their environment,
> by intuitive, 'instinctive perception,' which may come by experiencing all of the above,
> a 'speed up' of what has become memory, or perhaps it comes to us genetically as a genetic gift?

In this final article, and in the unpublished notes of his final lecture, Royston described landscape architecture as "preventive medicine" and its practitioners as able to "restore a marsh, purify the air, abate noise, provide systems in the city where trees will grow and people gather, exercise and laugh."[86]

Royston's favorite metaphor for a landscape architect was "physician of the landscape." It aptly describes his career. Practicing as a landscape surgeon, with teams of colleagues in his large corporate offices, he performed bold and skillful operations. By healing the postwar American city with intelligent design work, he hoped to foster healthy ecosystems, community spirit, and social justice.

In 1992, Royston knew it was unlikely he would ever write a book, but in a letter to a colleague he summarized the essence of his design approach: "When and if I ever had time to get to a book, I would integrate the real and implied spatial intent by abstracting the content of any space in order to test, to explain, to prove that all space has two- and three-dimensional form and space determinants that affect use, feeling and movement. That line, texture, mass, size, scale, color, smell, sound, edges, taste, etc. all play a part in spatial content and understanding the observed and implied. This philosophy has been the foundation of all design work I have ever done."[87]

Instead of writing, Royston spent his time experiencing the landscape and studying its effects on people. He maintained a straightforward yet subtle understanding of space. For him, spaces were not voids but engaging volumes defining the context of human life. Whether they were enjoying a garden, strolling in a park, or participating in a civic event in a public plaza, Royston asked people to relate to their surroundings. "Wherever you are, look around, feel it. How does the space affect your mind and body, how does it play with your senses? What are you seeing? What are the sounds? The smells? What are you physically touching? How many cultural connections or memories are suggested? What is the emotional response?"[88]

After his official retirement in 1995, Royston remained a consultant to his firm and to clients engaged in the restoration of his parks. In 2002, the city of Palo Alto embarked on a major renovation of Mitchell Park, and Royston served pro bono as consultant. As planners and citizens learned more about Royston's original design, the project shifted its focus from creating a new park to preserving a historic one. The eighty-eight-year-old Royston remembered thinking of the park as "a painting or sculpture. . . . Every shape, every form, relates to another. You can see it in an aerial view of the park."[89] During the course of the renovation, others also began to understand the value of the park's main playground in aesthetic terms. Adjustments were made for safety and financial feasibility, but the basic design of the playground remained in place, complete with the gopher holes inviting games of hide and seek and the beloved bear sculptures.

In the last two years of his life, Royston was commissioned by Brent Harris to design gardens for a pair of architecturally significant homes in Palm Springs, California. Royston responded with a sequence of gardens to surround a small guesthouse that was the product of Welton Becket's office (1960) and a larger home known as the Hefferlin house (1961) designed by the San Diego modernist Richard George Wheeler (figs. 28, 29). The Hefferlin house includes significant additions by the Swiss-born architect Albert Frey which influenced Royston's arrangement for the new gardens. Describing this final commission as "the garden I've been

Fig. 28. Becket guesthouse garden, Palm Springs, CA, 2017. Photo by Brent R. Harris.

waiting for," Royston revisited some of his most successful design innovations developed over the past sixty years. The design was a personal retrospective that synthesized forms taken from modern art, such as Kandinsky's *Several Circles,* and Cubist elements used in earlier residential projects such as the Naify garden. His proposal for the Hefferlin house pool included large circular floats he called "lily pads" to continue the garden's circular motif and reinforce the painterly reference.

Although Royston's eyesight was diminished at this time, his sense of proportion and scale were still keen, so for the large pool he specified custom-made oversize concrete coping and generously scaled waterline tile in a glaze created by his late friend the artist Edith Heath. The windscreens created for the Standard Oil Rod & Gun Club Park were reprised in the Becket garden, along with curvilinear turf plantings similar to those originally created for Mitchell

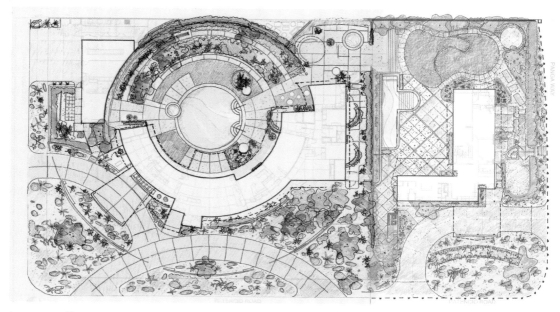

Fig. 29. Hefferlin-Becket site plan concept sketch, 2007. RHAA.

Park. His elegant garden tables at Mitchell Park which seem to float above the ground also made an appearance, this time in terrazzo. A fitting testament to Royston's genius, the Harris gardens preserve elements of his unique contribution to modern landscape design.[90]

Royston understood landscape architecture as "the fine art of relating the structure of culture to the nature of landscape, to the end that people can use it, enjoy it, and preserve it."[91] As a practitioner of this fine art he received many awards and distinctions, including membership in the Council of Fellows of the American Society of Landscape Architects (1975), the American Institute of Architects medal (1978), the Award of Honor in Landscape Architecture of the City of San Francisco Art Commission (1980), Honorary Fellow of the Australian Institute of Landscape Architecture (1986), and the American Society of Landscape Architecture Medal (1989), the highest award of that professional association.[92]

After a brief period of declining health, Robert Royston died at his home in Mill Valley on September 19, 2008. He chose to live and work in the Bay Area for his entire career—

Robert Royston, c. 1990. RHAA.

planning residential gardens, neighborhoods, recreation parks, and urban spaces. Although his firm had commissions in many states and countries, Royston's primary focus was always close to home. By maintaining this regional practice, he steadily built his landscape matrix. It may not have lived up to his ideal of a fully connected system of parks, plazas, and nature preserves, but, without a doubt, he contributed to making the Bay Area one of the country's most desirable locations to live and work. Through a practice based on improving the quality of life, Royston, as "physician of the landscape," designed landscapes to benefit community members of all ages, setting a high standard of inclusivity and environmental awareness that is even more relevant today.

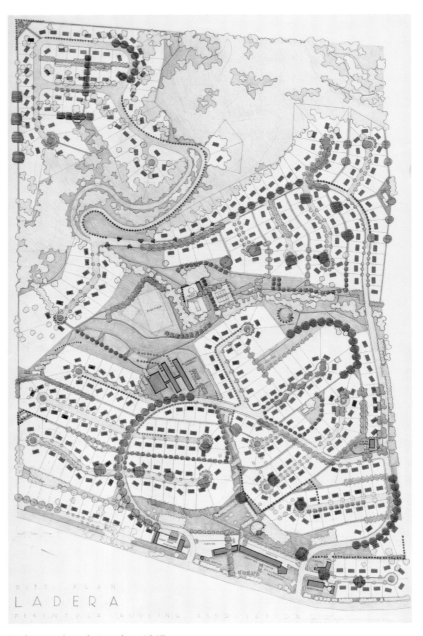

Ladera, colored site plan, 1947. RC EDA.

LADERA

SAN MATEO COUNTY, CALIFORNIA

1945–1949

Although the Ladera cooperative housing project was only partially implemented, the plan Eckbo, Royston & Williams created for it was an achievement of lasting importance for the fledgling firm. The collaborative experience of envisioning a new community within idyllic natural surroundings appealed to ERW's vision for the Bay Area and gave Royston his first opportunity to experiment with the "landscape matrix" as a panacea for the unprecedented and haphazard postwar development throughout the region. Eckbo and Royston began work on the plan in 1945, but when Eckbo left to open the firm's Los Angeles office the next year, Royston took on full responsibility for the details, including the playground designs and the fine-tuning of grading and planting plans.[1]

The inspiration for the project came from a group of young, idealistic Stanford University academics led by biochemistry professor James Murray Luck. In 1945, Luck and his colleagues formed the Peninsula Housing Association (PHA) to create a new community in the hills of San Mateo County, just a short drive from Palo Alto. These like-minded intellectuals established the social parameters of the development, accepting other, less upwardly mobile potential neighbors and welcoming racial diversity. From the beginning, the PHA focused on the land—the name "Ladera" means hillside in Spanish—and on dwelling in close association with nature, surrounded by native chaparral and enjoying spectacular views of the Bay Area.[2]

The author Wallace Stegner, an early member of the PHA, recalled that the cooperative "had the spirit that used to animate barn raisings when democracy was younger and simpler."[3] *Your Home in Ladera,* a promotional brochure published by the PHA, featured a cartoon of an airplane pilot, industrial worker, academic (in full regalia), businessman, cowboy, and female executive—all grouped around a landscape plan. The brochure decried the "cracker-barrel" housing and poorly designed communities typical of the rapidly expanding Bay Area. As a cooperative, Ladera's "democratic community" would offer convenient, affordable housing in the country, without the social isolation of a rural location.[4]

The PHA chose Eckbo, Royston & Williams to produce its ideal plan and hired the architects Joseph Allen Stein and John Funk, along with the engineer Joseph Cirino, to design their homes. The collaboration between this close-knit group of friends and colleagues, and the blessing of their visionary clients, resulted in an innovative model plan for cooperative living. The program for Ladera, based in part on questionnaires distributed to PHA members, called for single-family houses for about four hundred families on a 260-acre site near Palo Alto. The site was beautiful but challenging. Its rolling topography, thickly wooded with mature live oaks, offered dramatic views of many of the Bay Area's landmarks—Mount Tamalpais, Mount Diablo, Mount Hamilton, Black Mountain, and the Santa Clara Valley. A winding valley split the site in half, making road alignment and house siting difficult. The hilly terrain included a plateau on the east side and a smaller one in the northwest cor-

Ladera model, 1947. JCM.

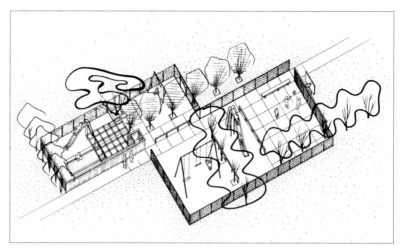

Playground studies, 1947.
RC EDA.

Concept sketches of homes and landscapes, 1947. RC EDA.

ner, accessible via a steep slope. Eckbo would later describe "similar but smaller plateaus" in the west half, "from which one climbs steeply through oak woods to an elevated knoll on which the more hide-away homes will be developed."[5]

The architectural plans of the homes were conceived in conjunction with the site plans, so that each house could be properly oriented on its lot. In January 1947, Funk and his associates were completing a topographic survey—mapping out two-foot contours on the building sites. At this point the site plan was expected to be finished by July, with construction beginning in 1948. During this period the PHA included 225 members.[6] Stein and Funk designed twelve different single-family residence plans employing modular wood-frame construction. The flat-roofed, one-story dwellings sold for $10,000 to $18,000 and were built on lots ranging from one-fifth to two-and-a-half acres. All had private

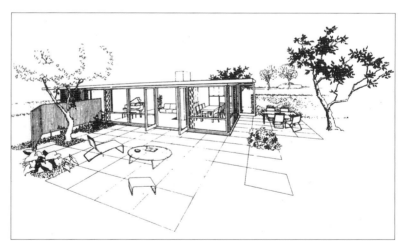

ABOVE AND OPPOSITE: House type Number Three: interior, view from patio, and floor plan with garden concept, from *Your Home in Ladera*, 1947.

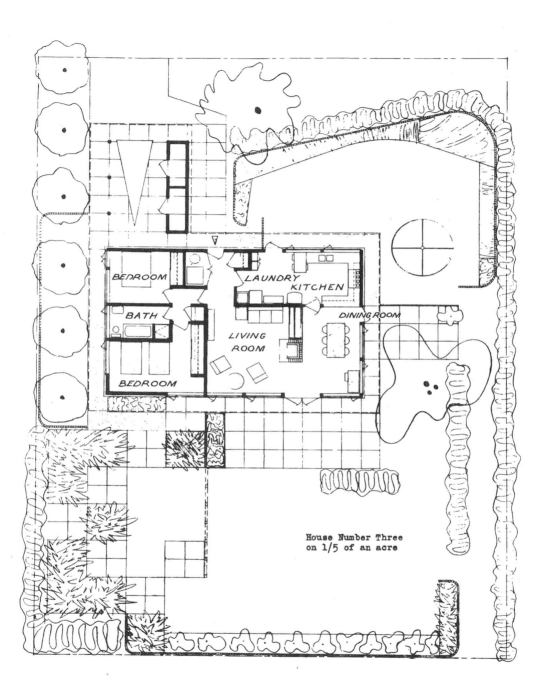

BEDROOM

LAUNDRY

KITCHEN

BATH

DINING ROOM

LIVING ROOM

BEDROOM

House Number Three
on 1/5 of an acre

gardens and were designed in a "California Contemporary" style intended to promote "pleasant, simple living."[7]

The design team responded to the site by laying down a circulation pattern that allowed for convenient access to the two plateaus offering the most suitable house sites. A loop road with twenty cul-de-sacs served the individual house lots, and careful alignment of the road system with the existing land contours minimized the need for grading. The curving valley functioned as a "landscape matrix" tying together the entire site plan and providing spaces for social interaction. The valley became a linear park containing the major recreation facilities—a community center with swimming pools for adults and children, tennis courts, a playground, and an elementary school. Pedestrian paths were laid throughout the park, which remained in its natural state of grassland and oak forest and connected with the school. Additional paths linking residences to the shopping center on the south perimeter formed the rest of the matrix. Most of these paths either ran between the rear lot lines or skirted the circular turning areas of the cul-de-sacs. It was possible to visit friends, walk to the school, drop by the recreation center, and shop for food without crossing a vehicular thoroughfare, a safety feature especially important for children.[8]

Each cul-de-sac was given a distinct street tree planting to establish its unique identity—a device Eckbo had used in some of his pre-war designs for the Farm Security Administration—and was sited in close proximity to one of the ten playgrounds for young children.[9] These playgrounds were designed by Royston and separated the spaces for children age one through four from those age five through eleven. He created additional playgrounds for older children in a circular form divided into quadrants to highlight specific activities.[10]

Although these playgrounds did not include the imaginative play equipment characteristic of Royston's later work, they did suggest his sensitivity to children's developmental needs, as well as the aesthetic and practical value of using planting design to create individualized spaces within a larger, unified playground. Ladera was envisioned as a small village of about sixteen hundred people living in single-family, detached residences. The plan also included a firehouse and a restaurant next to the small shopping center, as well as a guesthouse and an interdenominational chapel.

The Ladera dream eventually dissolved when the Federal Housing Authority denied the cooperative's request for a construction loan, most likely because Ladera was intended to be a racially integrated community. By 1949, only thirty-five houses had been constructed with individual financing, one house at a time.[11] The property was sold, and Eichler Homes developed its own plan for part of the site. For Royston, the experience of collaborating on Ladera was foundational, increasing his network of contacts and allowing him the freedom to experiment with a vision for urban planning that would become central to his career and to the long-term success of his firm.

View from hill behind Stein home with Royston home in background, Mount Tamalpais in distance, 1947. JCM.

ROYSTON AND STEIN GARDENS

MILL VALLEY, CALIFORNIA
1947–PRESENT

For over sixty years Robert Royston's garden in Mill Valley was his laboratory—an evolving testing ground for his ideas about planting, spatial composition, construction materials, and furniture design—as well as his most personal, private space. The garden accommodated a range of activities, from children's birthday parties to client presentations to afternoons of conversation over wine and a game of Pétanque. Such an outdoor lifestyle would become synonymous with California in the popular imagination by the latter half of the twentieth century, but in the immediate postwar period it was a concept just beginning to emerge from the work of a new generation of designers that included Robert Royston and his friend and colleague the architect Joseph Allen Stein.

Royston and Stein first met as members of Telesis, a progressive group of Bay Area designers, and in 1945 had begun collaborating on the Ladera cooperative housing project. A year later, the two embarked on the cooperative development of a property to accommodate their family homes. Stein discovered a hillside parcel in sparsely populated Marin County. The nearly three-acre site was on a wooded north-facing slope with views across the valley toward Mount Tamalpais, a regional landmark. Royston agreed that the lot was ideal, and planning for a pair of homes was begun. The gardens that resulted were remarkable, innovative designs that would influence modernist residential landscape architecture for decades to come.[1]

The Mill Valley property for the Royston and Stein homes was bounded by a street at the top of a slope on its south side and by irregularly shaped residential lots on all other sides. A short, fairly steep slope dropped from the street to a natural shelf, where the homes were sited, before resuming. Other homes in the vicinity were also set on this shelf, located by the dictates of topography rather than regard for property line setbacks. After a survey, Royston located the new buildings close to the center of the lot to allow for privacy and level space around them.

While designing the Royston and Stein residences, Royston was also commissioned to design two homes on a single lot in Berkeley for brothers Tom and Allen Hudson.[2] Unlike his site plan for the Hudson gardens, where a significant portion of the lot was used jointly by both families, the Royston and Stein households would have only the driveway and parking area in common. Automobile access to the property was only possible from the road above, a physical constraint that directed the site design. In response, Royston minimized the space required by designing a single driveway aligned perpendicular to the road. The driveway and auto circulation areas created a center line and a functional division of the property. Guided by a site plan that

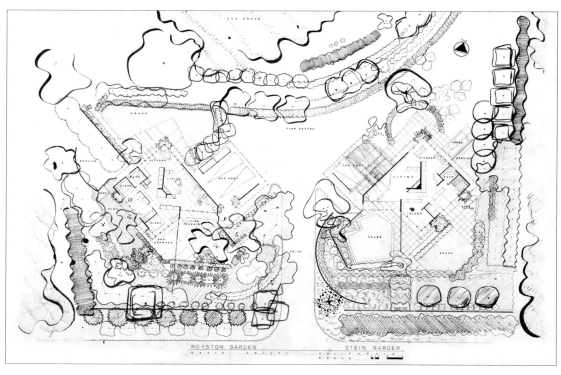

Concept plan of the two gardens, 1947. RC EDA.

provided privacy to both residences and took advantage of the views, Royston's grading scheme expanded the natural shelf by cutting into the uphill portion of the slope and filling the down slope areas to create level spaces for the gardens. This resulted in two roughly rectangular areas, each approximately fifty by seventy-five feet.

The collaboration with Royston on such a personal project enabled Stein to put his ideas about family housing into physical form. Since the late 1930s, while working in the Los Angeles office of Richard Neutra, he had designed modest, compact structures inspired by the work of this mentor and by Bay Area architect William Wurster.[3] The October

1940 issue of *Architectural Forum* included Stein's plan for a low-cost housing prototype with a series of spaces rotated forty-five degrees within a square building, an idea that he continued to develop after his move to the Bay Area in 1942.[4] That year, his plan for a low-cost, single-family home that resembled those he would build in collaboration with Royston was included in the San Francisco Museum of Art's *Houses for War and Post-War* exhibit.[5] The basic footprint was a square with a small angled extension, rotated forty-five degrees in relation to the road to create interesting angled garden spaces. A single flat roof plane covered the living space and extended over the adjacent parking area to form a carport, and deep overhangs sheltered predominantly glass walls. The living room, dining room, and kitchen, as well as adult and children's sleeping areas, all opened to patios and the gardens beyond.

In his plan for the landscape, Royston addressed the two gardens as a single design, but also emphasized the distinct character of each by developing subtle relationships between forms, both within each garden and between them. The gardens clearly illustrate his interest in translating the forms of early twentieth-century painting into three-dimensional compositions. At both houses, the entry sequence begins with a traditional-looking door that actually serves as a gate opening into a garden room. A freestanding panel wall, a repetition of the building's structural system, reinforces the hybrid nature of the space. The visitor moves through a walled area open to the sky before entering the building. Other walls of the houses are brought out into the landscape, generating more outdoor spaces without roofs. Royston's patio design reinforced the strategy by extending the ground plane with only the minimum drop in elevation necessary from the interior floor. Circulation

View of patio from bedroom, c. 1955. Photo by Ernest Braun, EBA.

patterns, zoning for use, and screening for privacy were fundamental issues considered by Royston when preparing his garden designs, but such program-generated concerns were only a starting point.

Royston's approach to planting design was informed by his background in painting and interest in sculpture. Black-and-white photographs impart the feeling that these early works were somber and reserved, but a series of articles in *Sunset* magazine describe the colorful planting combinations found in the first iteration of the Royston garden.[6] In the entry space, the freestanding concrete wall was painted dark blue to contrast with its pale yellow frame. The white spring bloom of the espaliered apple tree in front of the dark wall, and the honeysuckle vine trained against the thin slats of a gray screen, offered a vibrant seasonal display of color and complex contrasts of form and texture. Other dramatic plant combinations included dense purple-leafed plum paired with the airy gray foliage of bush germander, smooth European birch trees underplanted with the dark, rough bugleweed, and the needles of mugo or Swiss mountain pine contrasted with the flat soft leaves of dusty miller.

Although they were conceived as a single composition, the relationship between the Royston and Stein gardens began to change shortly after their creation. In 1952, Joseph Stein became head of the Department of Architecture at Bengal Engineering College in Calcutta, and although he returned from time to time to visit his former neighbors, he never lived in the house again. The property eventually passed into the hands of an owner who has acted as a thoughtful steward, effecting little change. Across the driveway, however, the Royston portion of the property reflects the consequences of decades of experimentation by one of the twentieth-century's most talented landscape architects.

The constraints of a limited construction budget prompted Royston to pursue imaginative design solutions and unusual choices of materials for his garden. Low retaining walls were made from surplus precast concrete laundry sinks, the play terrace was surfaced in redwood pieces obtained from a tree trimming company, and easily propagated placeholders such as geranium, iris, and agapanthus dominated in the planting plan. This first generation of the design included only a limited amount of concrete pav-

Children's play terrace surfaced in redwood bark, 1950. Photo by Ernest Braun, EBA.

ing. Rather, for the terraces adjacent to the house, Royston used a compacted aggregate called Haydite, a lightweight expanded shale product used in the construction of ship decks during World War II.[7] This sort of imaginative frugality was likely part of the public interest in the gardens, especially in California, where the ranks of veterans anxious to return to domestic life confronted a postwar housing shortage.

As Royston's garden changed over the years, the art screen wall separating the north garden from the laundry

View of Royston garden with Haydite paving and framework for garden screen, 1950. JCM.

Paved terraces on south side, c. 1955. Photo by Ernest Braun, EBA.

and service area remained prominent. Royston designed and built the screen to showcase sculptural tiles made by the artist Florence Alton Swift, whom he met while employed in Thomas Church's office.[8] In 1949, when Eckbo, Royston & Williams was asked to contribute to *Design in the Patio,* an exhibition at the San Francisco Museum of Art, Royston realized the art screen wall he had envisioned.[9] He built the screen and furniture for the exhibit at his new home in Mill Valley with the idea that all would return and become part of his garden. The screen project also gave Royston an opportunity to explore the use of Plexiglas, a new lightweight glass substitute, for garden construction. This suc-

Sketch of garden screen. From Eckbo, *Landscape for Living* (1950).

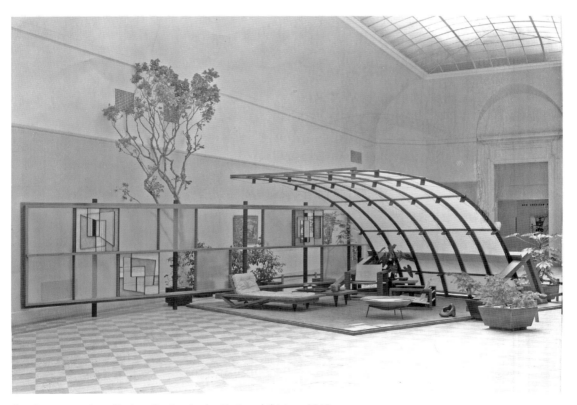

Garden screen installed at *Design in the Patio* exhibition, 1949. JCM.

North patio with Royston-designed chairs and table, c. 1955. Photo by Ernest Braun, EBA.

cessful interaction with a professional artist—Royston's first—led to collaborations on both private and public work with Claire Falkenstein, Benny Bufano, Ruth Asawa, and Henry Moore.

Over time, Royston's financial success enabled him to develop the garden along the lines originally imagined. A freestanding work room was added to the service yard. Concrete terraces were installed next to the house in areas that had been compacted aggregate paving. Permanent plantings replaced earlier placeholders. Beginning in 1955,

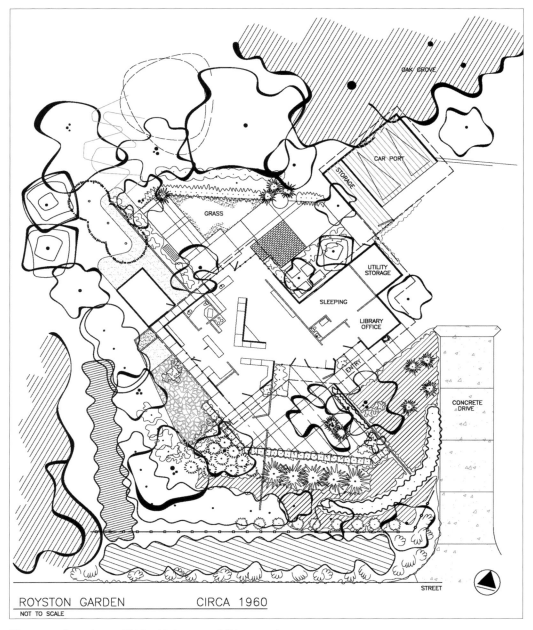

Within the image:
OAK GROVE
CAR PORT
STORAGE
GRASS
UTILITY STORAGE
SLEEPING
LIBRARY OFFICE
ENTRY
CONCRETE DRIVE
STREET
ROYSTON GARDEN   CIRCA 1960
NOT TO SCALE

Diagram of garden c. 1960 with house additions and carport. Drawn by JC Miller.

the house was expanded to accommodate the growing Royston family. The adjacent carport was enclosed to create a new bedroom suite for the parents and a new parking structure added at the bottom of the newly paved driveway. These changes created a courtyard space outside of the master bedroom with a greater sense of enclosure. With encouragement and help from their father, the Royston children colonized the down slope with ad hoc play forts and excavated caves. The orientation of the new carport and the addition of coast redwoods framed the northward view from the courtyard toward Mount Tamalpais.

The addition a decade later of an expansive deck with studio space—the capstone of the design—fully integrated the garden into the larger landscape, formalizing the desired connection between the garden and the mountain. Reached by three shallow steps, the nearly sixty-foot-long deck created a promontory with a dramatic view across the valley. The deck included built-in benches and tables, and a new design studio was tucked beneath it. Japanese maples and additional redwoods were planted. From this point, and over the next two decades, the paving, structures, and arrangement of the garden remained static, but plant growth and development of the tree canopy significantly altered the character of the place. Photos from the 1970s, the apex of Royston's professional career, show all parts of the garden in shade. Native oak and other plants had become large specimens, obscuring the plan's original spatial definition. By 1975, the art screen was completely enveloped in ivy, with small windows trimmed to expose the sculptural panels.

In the early 1990s, as Royston reduced his professional activity, he turned his attention to domestic projects. By removing overgrown trees, shrubs, and ivy, he brought

View of garden showing studio building below deck, 1972. Photo by Royston. JCM.

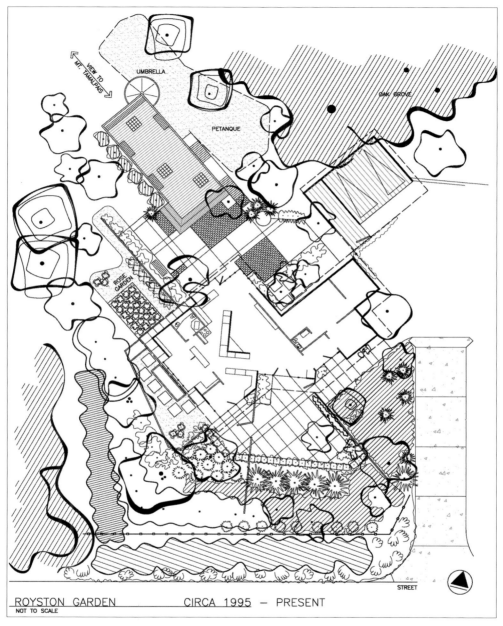

Labels within the diagram:
VIEW TO MT. TAMALPAIS
UMBRELLA
OAK GROVE
PETANQUE
ROSE GARDEN
STREET

ROYSTON GARDEN   CIRCA 1995 – PRESENT
NOT TO SCALE

Diagram of garden in 1995 showing tree removal. Drawn by JC Miller.

View of deck, 2006. Photo by JC Miller.

light back into his garden and revealed its structure. The decrepit workroom was removed, the slab foundation repurposed as a rose garden, and the art screen restored to prominence. The lowest portion of the garden was cleared and decomposed granite installed as a surface for outdoor games. One of Royston's signature disk-style garden umbrellas, hovering below the studio room, offered shade to his guests. This family garden is extraordinary in that it represents the original work of the practitioner as well as more than sixty years of his personal stewardship, and serves as a continuing exhibition of the design principles and artistic awareness Royston brought to hundreds of gardens, parks, and urban spaces.

Standard Oil Rod & Gun Club Park, adult and children's swimming pools, 1950. RC EDA.

STANDARD OIL ROD & GUN CLUB PARK

POINT RICHMOND, CALIFORNIA

1950

Royston's first major park commission, for the Standard Oil Rod & Gun Club, introduced some of his most innovative ideas about form, space, and the collaborative nature of design work. The Standard Oil refinery at Port Richmond commissioned the design, the site plan and program of which were developed in close consultation with company executives and workers; skilled welders and machinists completed much of the construction in their free time, without pay.[1]

The twenty-acre site fronted a small cove with a beach providing expansive views across San Francisco Bay to the north. Royston defined the park's entrance with a row of acacia trees on either side of the main road. A parking lot for two hundred cars was located on the western edge of the site, leaving as much space as possible free for pedestrians. Along the beachfront, Royston designed a complex of docks for recreational boating and a system of rock jetties. An encircling ridge of low hills divided by drainage swales formed the site's southern boundary. Mature coast live oak and elm, and other native vegetation such as ceanothus and manzanita, covered the hills and concealed any view of the refinery. Despite its proximity to the industrial facilities, the park seemed like a remote harbor.

Royston skillfully incorporated the existing landforms to create three distinct recreational zones linked by pedestrian paths. Two ridges projected at right angles from the

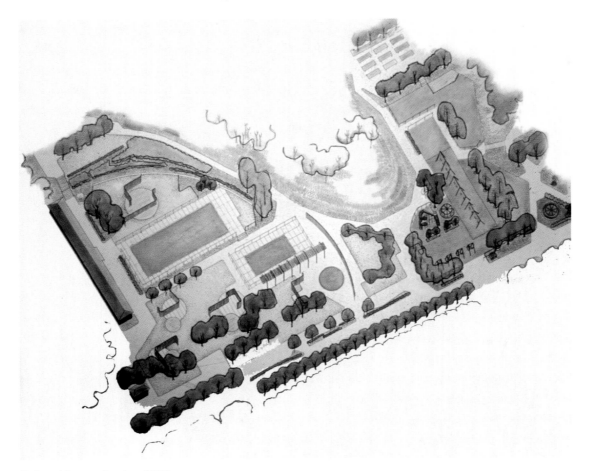

Colored isometric plan, 1950. JCM.

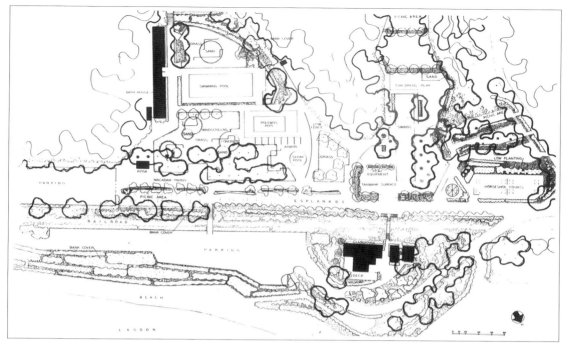

Site plan, 1950. RC EDA.

range of hills behind the park site to form three well-defined pockets facing north on the Bay. The easternmost of these was already occupied by a gymnasium, and Royston reinforced its spatial definition with a thick planting of elm and acacia. An existing swimming pool dominated the center space, and to the west was an open field. A straight road along the northern edge of the site led to the beach and the old clubhouse.

Two new recreation zones, framed by the projecting ridges of the middle and western sections of the park, formed a swimming area and a children's play area linked by a series of walkways. The swimming facilities were enlarged with a new wading pool for tots (the "Polywog Pool") and a swim-

View with wading pool, 1950. JCM.

ming pool for older children. Subtle level changes in the gently sloping site separated the three pool areas, and a series of overlapping walls of acacia trees added spatial definition. Whenever possible, Royston preserved existing mature elms in the vicinity of the pools. He also planted additional eucalyptus and elm on the projecting ridges to increase their effectiveness as windbreaks.[2]

Frequent dense fog and chilling winds were typical of the Bay Area, where one day might be fifty degrees and foggy, and the next sunny and much warmer. Royston accommodated these variations in climate with gracefully curving wooden screens to serve as windbreaks and sun traps for sunbathing, as well as steel pergolas with wooden slat roofs to shade the seating areas near the children's pool. A one-story building with dressing rooms formed the eastern boundary of the pool area. On the southern end of the site, at the base

Windscreens and sun traps, 1950. JCM.

Pool pergola, 1950. JCM.

of the surrounding hills, densely shaded picnic areas offered relief from the sun. This careful zoning, based on the recreational needs of various age groups, would become characteristic of Royston's park designs.

By using durable construction materials throughout the park, Royston reduced the need for maintenance, a cost-cutting factor of even greater importance in his later public parks. The ground plane in the sunbathing and pool areas was a mixture of turf, sand, and concrete slabs to provide users with various choices of surfaces for picnics or play. The slabs were cast in irregularly shaped arcs and rectangles. Pergolas and play equipment were made primarily of bent or welded steel fashioned by the metal workers. Royston's use of garden elements such as wooden fences and arbors gave the park a feeling of intimacy, almost as if the entire space were a residential patio and yard.[3]

The play area contained some of Royston's early designs for imaginative play equipment, a marked improvement on the standard features of his Ladera playgrounds. The centerpiece was a captivating twenty-five-foot-high spiral slide Royston claimed as the tallest piece of play equipment in the Bay Area.[4] He also created a version of a merry-go-round, with a revolving disk that generated centrifugal force and cast riders into a sandbox, as well as single and double swings designed with curved support structures. All the equipment was painted in bright colors and remains little changed. The closely spaced wooden pickets surrounding the play area allowed adults to comfortably rest their elbows while supervising children's play. The picnic grove in the southwest corner was furnished with a row of barbecue pits buffered from the parking lot to the west by a thick grove of elm and eucalyptus. A series of wall-like tree plantings subdivided the interior of this westernmost area, creating

Spiral slide, 1950. JCM.

the impression of a larger space and making the park feel less crowded. The planting plan for the site used vegetation to define spaces, a central component of Royston's design theory. He carefully preserved the existing native trees to form shade canopies and planted the walkways with low-maintenance, drought-resistant shrubs such as pyracantha, cytisus, and melaleuca for seasonal color and interesting textures.

Standard Oil Rod & Gun Club Park not only launched Royston's extensive park planning activity in the Bay Area but also received national attention in professional journals.[5] In the 1960s, Royston wrote a brief article about the park,

Play equipment, 1950. JCM.

Sandbox and wooden fences, 1950. JCM.

describing it as one of his favorite commissions.[6] He enjoyed collaborating with the refinery workers as well as applying the spatial ideas and details of his garden designs to a large-scale project.[7] The park's imaginative formal expression—its nonaxial spaces, creative accommodation of form to human use, understated details, and innovative play equipment—heralded new directions in the design of American parks.

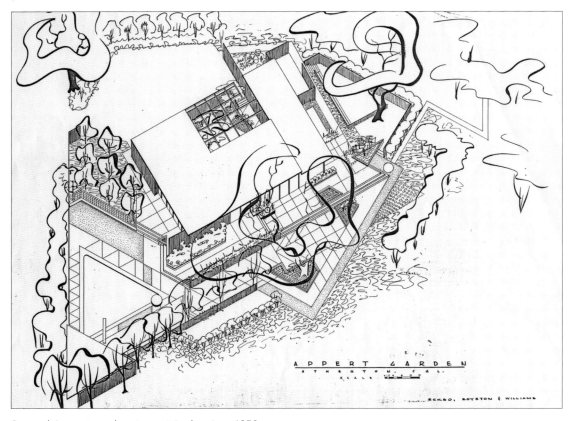

Second Appert garden, isometric drawing, 1952. RC EDA.

SECOND APPERT GARDEN

ATHERTON, CALIFORNIA

1950

In 1946, Royston received his first residential commission with the firm of Eckbo, Royston & Williams, a small garden for the Appert family sited on a steep hillside in San Francisco. The garden's low-maintenance planting plan and engaging Cubist-like angular forms pleased his clients, Kurt E. Appert, the founder of Lenkurt Electric Company, and Violet Appert, an amateur musician. Four years later, they called on Royston to design the landscape for a larger house on a spacious wooded lot in Atherton, on the San Francisco Peninsula; in 1959, Royston would design a garden for their retirement home.[1] The Apperts represented the type of creative, entrepreneurial clients prospering in the Bay Area, and their endorsement bolstered Royston's effort to develop a signature modernist style in garden design.

Based on Royston's recommendation, the Apperts hired the architect Joseph Stein to design their second house. They gave the team a free hand, making few requests other

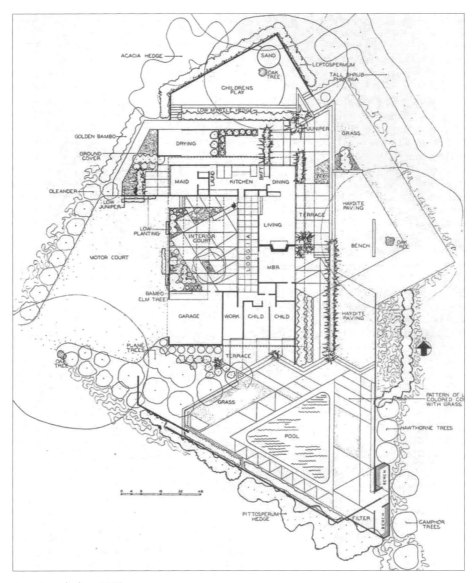

Annotated plan, 1952. RC EDA.

than a play area for their daughters and an ample terrace. The designers responded with a sophisticated integration of indoor and outdoor space that preserved the mature coast live oaks on the site and accommodated the family's routines. Royston and Stein took advantage of the awkward triangular shape of the lot by siting the house near its western border, where two roads flanking the parcel on the north and south converged to form the apex of the triangle. This decision opened up the rest of the lot for a spacious garden terrace and allowed for preservation of much of the remaining forest. A single large live oak became the focal point of the landscape. Throughout the commission, Royston and Stein constantly exchanged ideas, working together to

House with live oak, 1953. Photo by Ernest Braun, EBA.

Enclosed entry patio, 1953. Photo by Ernest Braun, EBA.

ensure that house and garden functioned as a seamless whole of interior and outdoor spaces.

The driveway led to a spacious auto court at the rear of the house. A long wall flanked by garage doors on one end and a small entry portal on the other opened to a bright and airy enclosed patio capped by an ivy-covered trellis. The entrance to the house was through a roofed, glass-enclosed "loggia" forming the rear wall of the patio. The loggia served as a hallway to the private living areas and as a playroom for the Apperts' two daughters. Stein's floor plan for the one-story 2,750-square-foot dwelling took advantage of the sloping site to divide the house into three levels—the entry patio and private living areas, the living and dining room, and a multilevel garden terrace—all connected by short flights of stairs. The living and dining area opened through sliding glass doors to the lower portion of the terrace, which extended along three sides of the house. The floors were the same color concrete as most of the large rear terrace, creating the impression that the living and dining room flowed outside, separated only by a thin glass membrane. The master bedroom on the west side of the house and the two bedrooms for the children on the south side opened to the upper level of the terrace, a more private realm.

On the north side of the house Royston created a small kitchen garden for the housekeeper and a play area. He also planted a row of trees and understory shrubs outside the seven-foot wooden fence along the south boundary as a buffer against traffic noise and to provide privacy for the swimming pool, which was almost flush with the southern lot line. The multilevel terrace wrapping around the rear facade and extending along the north and south elevations of the house became the major feature of the garden as well. Concrete square and triangular pavers separated by thin redwood joints

Swimming pool, 1953. Photo by Ernest Braun, EBA.

formed the ground plane of the terrace. Its plinthlike concrete construction consisted of a series of sharply angled polygons and triangles forming a visual contrast to the horizontal lines of the house. A seating area extended the full length of the facade at the same level as the living and dining rooms. As Royston recalled, the Apperts liked the unconventional, triangle-shaped pool on the lower level and "didn't mind swimming in circles."[2] While the pool's unusual shape harmonized with the rest of the terrace's sharp angularity, it was also a necessary accommodation to the awkward slant of the property line on the south side. The square footage of the garden terrace and enclosed entry patio was almost twice that of the house, a dramatic announcement of the pleasures of outdoor living. Because the terrace edges were almost parallel with the natural contours of the ridge, minimal grading was required.

Throughout his landscape design, Royston used color to create a unified composition and ease the transition from indoors to outdoors. The triangular pavers echoed the pool's equilateral triangle and were arranged in a row of alternating hues of red and gray, the red coordinating with the living room's Roman brick walls. Royston chose aqua blue for the forty-eight-foot-long wooden planter and the wooden mullions of the sliding-glass doors. A white concrete planter

Terrace, 1953. Photo by Ernest Braun, EBA.

Model showing spatial relationships, 1952. JCM.

just outside the living room paralleled the white band along the length of the roof. He softened the terrace's large area of concrete paving with a bosque of trees on its southern portion, beds of shrubs and flowers, and a twenty-five-foot-long raised wooden planter on the eastern section. The pool area featured a small lawn for sunbathing, and Royston planted the forested area beyond the terrace to the east with a carpet of grass. The bold arc of trees connecting the terrace with the pool area shown in the model was not included in the final planting plan.

Royston would recall the second Appert garden as one of his most satisfactory collaborations with an architect.[3] His growing reputation as a gifted designer was enhanced by the attention given to the project in newspapers and design journals. The residence was featured on the cover of *House & Garden* and described by *San Francisco Chronicle* architecture critic Vance Bourjaily as "very livable and serenely handsome."[4] The subtle use of color, texture, and space to create a sense of visual and emotional balance—characteristic of this garden—was one of Royston's most significant contributions to modernist design.

Chinn garden, view of terrace from apartment above, 1951. Photo by Ernest Braun, EBA.

CHINN GARDEN

SAN FRANCISCO

1951

In 2006, when asked to choose a favorite among his many residential garden designs, Royston replied without hesitation, "the Chinn garden."[1] Both a captivating abstract composition and a place in which a large family could relax in the midst of the city, the Chinn garden exemplified Royston's lifelong effort to incorporate modern art into daily life. The small garden was located at the rear of a four-story apartment building on the edge of San Francisco's Chinatown. Royston recalled the client, A. B. Chinn, a local physician who owned the building, as a quiet man who had few requests beyond wanting to replace the existing nondescript garden with something better. Since the Chinn family occupied the fourth floor of the building, which offered a clear view of the site, Royston saw an opportunity to create a three-dimensional abstract design to be appreciated from above. The garden would also become an outdoor living space for the Chinns and their young children and serve as a sun trap, offering shelter from the cold winds characteristic of the area.[2]

Royston removed all traces of the former landscape except for one mature loquat tree and enclosed the area with a seven-foot-high wooden fence of square posts and thin, closely spaced horizontal cross pieces. This screen provided privacy from the adjacent apartment buildings. The garden was entered from the rear of the building by a short flight of steps or a ramp, both of which were bordered with Hahn's ivy and St. John's wort. A narrow passageway along the side of the building, flanked with alternating rectangular beds of fulsia and aurea, connected the garden to the street. The passageway was paved with Haydite, a lightweight aggregate shale product developed for ship construction during the war. Small trees in single rows along the sides and rear of the garden and four border beds of sedum and ivy formed a green frame around the central section. The left border was a line of eucalyptus; black poplar were planted in the right and rear borders.

The central section of the garden, comprising 90 percent of its area, was paved in pastel-colored rectangular Haydite pavers of varying dimensions. To add textural variety Royston specified coarse Haydite for some pavers and fine for others. Dwarf shrubs and groundcovers such as ajuga, box, sedum, festuca, ivy, and cryptomeria were interspersed within the paving pattern. All plants in the central area were placed in small rectangular beds drilled into the pavers, and when seen from above appeared to have sprung from the Haydite surface. A row of five small *Cryptomeria japonica* 'Globosa Nana' and another of five moss sawara cypress, planted in straight lines and trimmed in spherical shapes, added variety and movement to the visual pattern. Royston increased the three-dimensional effect of the plantings by positioning a square wooden arbor with a semitransparent roof off-cen-

View of arbor and wooden fence, 1951. Photo by Royston. JCM.

View across garden, 1951. Photo by Royston. JCM.

ter in the composition. The cross members forming the roof were spaced just wide enough to reveal the paving pattern underneath when seen from above. The arbor also served as a convenient place for family dining.

The square and rectangular pavers, separated from one another by thin strips of redwood painted black, were pastel pink, orange, and purple grouped around the perimeter, with light gray filling out the composition, and small areas of yellow serving as accents. This ground plane of harmonious forms and colors drew the eye around the perimeter and then to the center. The multicolored design created a visual experience of figure-ground reversal similar to an op art painting. Royston even color coordinated the garden's butterfly chairs (icons of the 1950s) to match the pink of the pavers. He also included a chair of his own design with a rectangular wooden

A Royston-designed chair included in the garden, 1951. Photo by Ernest Braun, EBA.

frame that echoed the shape of the Haydite pavers. By using a family of similar forms and a carefully chosen color combination, Royston created a pleasing balance of visual effects within a unified composition.

Royston's colleague at the University of California, Berkeley, Steven C. Pepper, described the ideal contemporary garden as "an abstract painting for people to live within."[3] Royston agreed, and the Chinn garden realized that vision. His clients appreciated the garden's aesthetics and enjoyed its functional elements. The large Haydite surface allowed a generous area for play, and the central open space was ideal for outdoor entertaining. The low-maintenance garden required little other than watering the hardy plants, sweeping the pavers, and pruning the cryptomeria and cypress. *Sunset* magazine praised the garden for its "color and texture," and architect Richard Neutra featured it as an example of the modernist "patio house" in an article for *House and Garden*.[4]

KRUSI PARK PLAYGROUND

ALAMEDA, CALIFORNIA

1954

After visiting the Standard Oil Rod & Gun Club playground in the early 1950s, Alameda park administrators came away wanting something similar for an existing five-acre park in a residential neighborhood on the island of Alameda, across the bay from San Francisco. The playground site was adjacent to a small kindergarten, typical of the park-school combination popular with urban planners and advocated by the American Public Health Association.[1] Park officials called for the usual sandbox, wading pool, and standard play equipment, but Royston took their program merely as a point of departure, expanding it with highly original formal and spatial arrangements as well as inventive play equipment.

In plan, Royston's design for the Krusi Park playground reads like a carefully composed abstract sculpture. Circular and amoeba-like shapes are layered on a gridded concrete ground plane. A curvilinear six-foot-high wall of wooden palings encloses the area, separating it from the rest of the park. The semitransparent fence affords glimpses of the children and facilitates their supervision. Openings in the inwardly curving portions of the fence define its two entrances, an example of "line" used to suggest movement through space, a key aesthetic principle of Royston's design theory.

Royston's playground was one of the first based on his generation's new ideas about the nature of play. The 1940s and 1950s were a period of innovation in playground design, with articles in such well-respected periodicals as *Architectural*

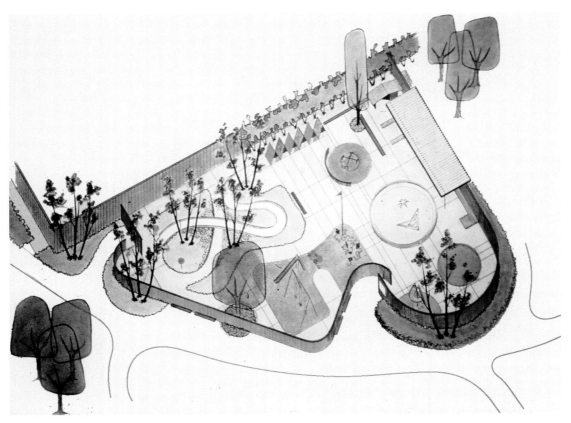

Krusi Park playground, colored isometric sketch for "Tiny Tot Area," 1954. RC EDA.

Record calling for the use of modern sculpture as a form of play equipment.[2] During the planning phase of the Krusi Park commission, Royston began to observe children playing in order to design equipment that would both stimulate the imagination and encourage challenging physical activity. His theories not only evolved from his childhood experiences and those of his own children but also responded to commercial efforts to entertain children in parklike settings, such as Fairyland, in nearby Oakland. When Fairyland opened in 1950, it welcomed children with well-known storybook characters, such as Snow White and the Seven Dwarfs and the Old Woman Who Lived in a Shoe, who talked when a key was inserted in a slot.[3] Royston's park would avoid such imagery, and its predetermined associations that inhibited children's imaginations, by offering play structures in abstract forms that children could incorporate into their own fantasies. A series of raised, sawed-off tree trunks forming a path might become a passage across a swamp filled with exotic creatures or a challenging route through treetops. Not doctrinaire, Royston also included representational equipment in the form of a pedal car freeway.

Like the Ladera and Rod & Gun Club playgrounds, the Krusi design was carefully zoned to accommodate children of different ages. The west end, with its irregular gridded concrete paving, contained a cluster of circular play areas, a wading pool, a sand area, and a wooden playhouse resembling the post-and-beam architecture of the surrounding neighborhood. An additional shade trellis, small spiral slide, and simple climbing structure completed the area. The trellis, with its long bench, allowed parents to socialize while supervising their children. The climbing structure, sand area, and wading pool were carefully spaced just far enough apart to avoid congestion but close enough to allow a child

Concrete climbing structure, 1954. JCM.

to move easily from one to another. The sand areas had a stepped curb to keep the sand contained and included an inviting concrete play mountain in the center. In keeping with his theory that design was intuitive, rather than making a working drawing for the mountain, Royston met the construction crew on the day it was poured and supervised the sculpting of its form spontaneously, a type of improvisation he enjoyed in his playground work.[4]

The east end of the playground catered to older children. Its paving was gridded in a different scale to mark it

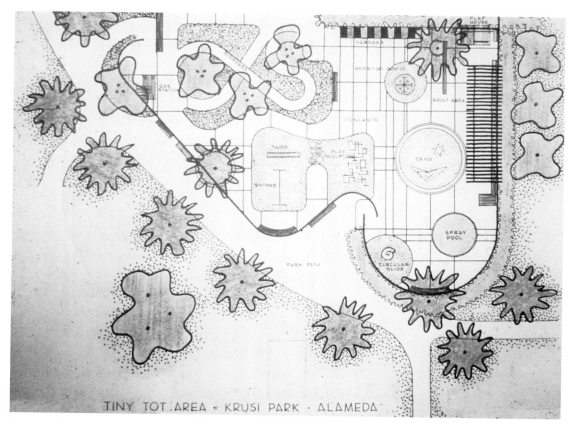

Annotated plan for "Tiny Tot Area," 1954. JCM.

Custom-made pipe climbing structure and pedal car freeway, 1954. JCM.

off from the west area. A colorful sculpture composed of pipes, by the artist Raymond Rice, exemplified the idea of play structure as "art." Nearby, a row of tree stumps, a larger slide, and a vertical concrete climbing slab were arranged with an intention that children would link these features in imaginary play. The main feature of the east section was the large freeway-like ramp for pedal cars. These were housed in a row of adjacent A-frame garages, which were locked at night. The ramp had a tight S-curve on the downgrade to test the skill of the adventurous driver; the risk Royston incorporated into this experience was more perceived than actual since a curb kept cars from careening over the edge. A small gas station at the foot of the ramp allowed motorists to fill up for the next run. This encouraged children to play gas station attendant—cooperative play that Royston believed

Pedal car garages, 1954. JCM.

Gas station, 1954. JCM.

was essential to a child's ability to develop good relationships with peers.

Shortly after the playground's completion, a kindergarten teacher remarked to Royston, "This is the only place around here where children don't cry."[5] Royston knew better, but the continuing heavy use of the playground was testament to its success. Krusi Park was described in the San Francisco Museum of Modern Art's *Landscape Architecture 1958* exhibition catalog as "an experiment with imaginative space."[6] Although the park remains, its original playground no longer exists, the victim of reduced maintenance budgets and fears of litigation.

Mitchell Park, presentation model, 1956. JCM.

MITCHELL PARK

PALO ALTO, CALIFORNIA
1956

After Royston completed the Rod & Gun Club Park in 1954, Palo Alto officials invited him to design an eighteen-acre park on the city's suburban fringe. The flat site, a former wheat field, was chosen for its proximity to two new elementary schools on its west border, a middle school on the south, and a branch library to the east.[1] The Palo Alto planners promoted the "park-school concept" based on a new government manual for park planning, which called for "community parks" to serve several clusters of neighborhoods.[2] Meadow Park, as it was initially named, would not only meet these expectations but ultimately become one the first modernist parks to serve the needs of the growing Bay Area suburbs.

From its earliest planning stages, Royston conceived of Mitchell Park as a public garden and understood the progressive social implications of this type of commission. He drew the scale and program of the new park from *Guide for*

Planning Recreation Parks in California, a study he helped shape through recommendations to its publication committee.[3] In addition to design guidelines, the publication mentioned much of the play equipment Royston would include—"gopher holes, wheel-toy freeway, and play sculptures"—as well as a concrete slab for skating and dancing, a parklike area for free play, a natural area, and a community center. Royston kept a copy of the publication in his office and used these accepted, widely distributed guidelines as a point of departure for discussion with citizens and municipal authorities.

Skating on the multi-use slab, 1956. JCM.

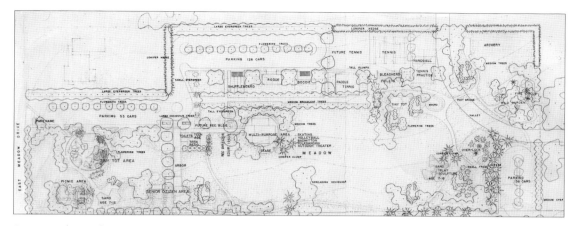

Annotated site plan, 1955. RC EDA.

As a landscape architect, he had little or no control over the size and location of his park commissions, decisions dictated by city governments, but he transformed the standard expectations for playgrounds and recreational spaces with his creative, modernist design theory.

The simple plan of Mitchell Park reflected its purpose—to serve all visitors by offering a range of opportunities for outdoor recreation. A clear circulation system, consisting of a main axis and a cross axis, anchored the spaces within the park and gave easy access to its many recreational areas. The main north-south axis was partially formed by the straight, tree-lined entry drive and the parking area conveniently sited near the "tiny tot playground." Halfway into the park, this road became a walkway flanked by mimosa trees, which terminated at a fountain. Adjacent to this north-south axis and connected to it by a series of paths were facilities serving different age groups—the tiny tot playground, a shuffleboard court, and a paddle tennis area. Across a creek in the far southeast corner of the park were a wild garden shaded by redwoods offering a quiet retreat and a small archery range.

Colored isometric drawing of "tiny tot playground," 1955. RC EDA.

The spine of the park, its north–south axis, joined the east–west axis near a one-story multi-use building. This community center included a meeting room, a lounge for teenagers, and the office of the recreation director, whose job was to plan and coordinate various park activities ranging from art classes to team sports. The east–west cross axis, sheltered by a wisteria arbor, terminated an area catering to older adults, equipped with horseshoe pitches, chess tables, a picnic area, and a putting green.

To create spatial variety and divide areas by use, Royston shaped the site with a series of landforms made from soil excavated for a city sewer project. He created five-foot turf-covered berms to separate the children's play area from the seniors' facilities and to screen a parking area at the south

Presentation sketch of "Senior Citizen Area" with picnic arbor, 1955. JCM.

Picnic arbor, 2014. Photo by Dillingham Associates Landscape Architecture.

Screen and berms at picnic area, c. 1970. JCM.

Multi-use slab, 2014. Photo by Dillingham Associates Landscape Architecture.

end of the park. Three-foot berms enclosed the tiny tot playground and the circular theater / skating rink to the south, but no berms separated the twelve acres of playing fields to the west, which were officially outside the park. This strategy of borrowing scenery by creating vistas outside the park boundaries made the new park appear much larger. The final design, with over twenty-eight features, would include a wild garden, numerous picnic areas, playing fields, and special equipment for outdoor games. This mixture of opportunities for active and passive recreation for all ages expressed Royston's ideal for the public park.

The tiny tot area featured some of Royston's most imaginative play equipment. "The apartment house," a multistory structure of stacked wire mesh cubes connected by a ladder, allowed children to experience height without the need for close supervision. This play structure exemplified Royston's belief that experiencing sensations of risk, height, and free movement are important to child development. The amoeba-like wading pool was specially designed so that its depth decreased as a young child ventured from the edge toward its center, further removed from adult supervision. Perceived risk was heightened, but actual risk was minimal. Royston's "gopher holes," cut into a hollow concrete slab set into an earthen berm, invited children to disappear underground and pop up elsewhere, accommodating the need for concealment and surprise and encouraging group play. Royston also designed another version of the pedal car freeway, so successful at Krusi Park. The local fire department kept the cars in working order and locked them in their garages at night. Along with the requisite climbing bars, swings, and a large sand area, the playground featured local artist Virginia Green's concrete bear sculptures, whose highly textured surfaces invited climbing.[4] The Palo Alto park planners

Apartment house climbing structure, 1956. JCM.

Wading pool renovated as splash pad, 2005. Photo by Reuben Rainey.

"Gopher holes," 1956. JCM.

Pedal car freeway, 1956. JCM.

working with Royston recognized the exceptional nature of his design, characterizing it as "novel," "modern," and "embodying the creative living theme."[5]

Royston believed in the restorative power of contact with nature, and his planting plan for Mitchell Park was lush, with a variety of trees and shrubs chosen to define space and provide visual interest throughout the seasons.[6] He paid special attention to leaf texture and growth habit in his selections, using redwoods to mark the corners of the park and provide points of orientation; other trees at

Concrete bear sculpture, 2005. Photo by Reuben Rainey.

Picnic arbor with horse chestnuts in bloom, 2008. Photo by Charles Birnbaum.

the park's two main axes created low ceilings and shaded seating areas.

At Mitchell Park, Royston employed a consistent design vocabulary, adjusting the details of each space based on its size and function. In more formal areas, pergolas painted Chinese red (his favorite color) were positioned to cast shadow patterns on the pavements. All seating and light fixtures were custom designed.[7] The smaller playgrounds employed a rich array of complex forms that children could readily identify at close range, as the scale was similar to that of a large residential garden. In the larger, meadow-like center of the park, however, Royston took a different approach utilizing a less complex geometry. His tree walls read clearly and created a free-flowing spatial continuum down the spine of the entire park, tying together its various components. Picnic areas and playgrounds were distributed to avoid the monotony of single-use zones and invite users to explore the far corners of the park. When he analyzed the "big picture," Royston stepped away from the details to create interlocking abstract forms that not only were functional and without precedent at this scale but also resulted in a well-designed and easily navigable park.

In *A Community Park,* a short documentary film created by RHAA in 1961, Royston introduced a new kind of park aimed at the needs of the family.[8] The film asked communities to come together and collaborate with "their design assistants" on parks to serve their growing suburban neighborhoods. The urgency for open space was particularly clear in the Palo Alto area, where building was taking place "very quickly and much too close together." Little privacy and no open space led to questions of safety. Mitchell Park would serve as a public refuge from the encroaching suburbs—a place where all ages could find space to engage in recreation and social interaction. As his film illustrates, Royston's ideas about parks as public gardens had become a political statement by the early 1960s. Mitchell Park was his manifesto on the public right to open space and the potential for such public gardens to foster community spirit, as well as his own ethical commitment to bring order and amenity to the rapidly expanding and often poorly planned suburbs.

Royston's film about the need for Mitchell Park ended with a humble statement: "One community did this—it took about a year—it has proven its worth." Over forty years later, Royston returned to the park as a consultant on its restoration. Today, Mitchell Park is a testament to the city's prescient planning as well as to the enduring quality of Royston's design. The park not only continues to prove its worth but now also includes a Magical Bridge playground, a new accessible play area for disabled children designed by RHAA and completed in 2016.

St. Mary's Square, view of park from upper floor of adjacent building, 1957. JCM.

ST. MARY'S SQUARE

SAN FRANCISCO

1957

In the 1950s, public squares atop parking garages were a new phenomenon of the emerging automobile landscape, along with drive-in theaters and restaurants and drive-through banks and even churches. Royston's first major inner-city commission was a large parking garage on the southeast edge of Chinatown, just west of the financial district. St. Mary's Square, the second city square designed for the roof of a parking garage in the San Francisco area, was just half a mile from Union Square (1942), the first such example in North America.[1]

The city commissioned the project to relieve an acute parking shortage in one of the most densely populated areas of the city. A massive undertaking by the City and County of San Francisco Recreation and Parks Commission and the City of San Francisco Parking Authority, the reinforced concrete parking garage was carved out of the steep hillside between Pine and California Streets. From the beginning of the proj-

Sketch of park plaza, 1957. JCM.

ect, in 1953, Royston collaborated with the architect Rudolf Igaz and the engineer John J. Gould to integrate the structural system of the garage with the design of the rooftop square over the fifth level. The garage was partially operative by 1954, and the square was completed three years later as the final phase of construction. The five-story structure accommodated over a thousand cars, as well as a small gas station, a car wash area, administrative offices, restrooms, waiting rooms, and a snack bar. Escalators connected all floors of the 55,000-square-foot structure and accessed the square on the fifth-floor level.[2] A small portion of the land for the square and parking garage was donated by St. Mary's Cathedral, whose sanctuary bordered the site on California Street. The cathedral's parcel—a small terraced park at the far western edge of the site—was replaced by the public space over the parking garage, which was named to honor its donor. Royston's design for the new square preserved portions of this original park, including a row of mature Lombardy poplars along its western border that formed a backdrop for the focal point of the new square—a twelve-foot statue of the Chinese patriot and statesman Sun Yat-sen by the sculptor Beniamino Bufano.[3]

In designing the 128-by-272-foot square, Royston

View across park from above, 1957. RHAA.

Sun Yat-sen statue, 2017. Photo by JC Miller.

San Francisco skyline from the park, 1957. JCM.

accommodated the garage's grid structure of reinforced concrete columns. Concrete tree planters were sited directly
above supporting columns on the fifth level. Areas of lawn
and shrubs were also carefully located in a twenty-inch
layer of topsoil, beneath which four inches of gravel ensured
drainage. A waterproof membrane covered by three inches
of concrete protected the ceiling of the garage.[4] Rather than
echoing the geometry of the underlying structural grid with
a checkerboard of walks, seating areas, and planters, Royston
worked closely with Gould to design curving lawn areas
recalling the biomorphic forms of his residential gardens. He
regarded these shapes as restful, a quality he hoped to instill
in crowded public spaces like St. Mary's Square.[5] Residents
of Chinatown found the space a welcome relief from the
commercial streets thronged with tourists.

The square is crossed by three twenty-foot-wide walkways paved with precast concrete slabs and bordered by lawn. One east-west walkway forms a central axis focusing on the statue of Sun Yat-sen set on a plinth. Despite Royston's personal reservations about iconography in his design work, here he readily accepted a statue that expressed historical and cultural values relevant to Chinatown.[6] Bufano's imposing mixed-media work, with its granite head and stainless steel garment modeled after a

View to St. Mary's Cathedral, 2017. Photo by JC Miller.

Turf areas and pavers, 2017. Photo by JC Miller.

Pine Street entry, 1957. JCM.

traditional Chinese gown, presides over the square with a commanding dignity.

In addition to the main system of three walkways, two smaller walks wind behind and around the statue and others connect with the raised lawn and tree areas. The pavers are squares or rectangles in slightly varying shades of gray that complement the turf areas. Visual interest is created through the contrast between the crisp forms of the pavers and the curvilinear concrete edges of the lawn areas. These edges vary in height from ten to fourteen inches and serve as continuous seating walls for large crowds; wooden benches are also scattered throughout the site. Square concrete tree planters with rounded corners, varying in height from two to three feet, interlock with the curving edges of the turf areas to accommodate large pittosporum and weeping cherry trees. A few turf areas are interspersed with drought tolerant, low-maintenance shrubs. To reinforce the soothing, cool color palette of the pavers, the planting design emphasizes textural variation. The areas of vegetation and paving are about equal, but the large trees make the planted areas appear more extensive. Royston sited additional concrete planting boxes at sidewalk level along the length of the garage on Pine and California Streets, giving a green edge to the imposing structure. This commission, one of Royston's last during his partnership with Garrett Eckbo and Edward Williams, strengthened his professional reputation in the Bay Area and helped his new firm, Royston, Hanamoto & Mayes, gain public projects in Alameda and on the Peninsula.

In the late 1990s, St. Mary's Square was restored and two children's playgrounds were added, along with restrooms. A bronze plaque commemorating the military service of Chinese Americans from San Francisco was relocated to a more prominent position near the central walk. Many of the original concrete pavers were replaced, but their form and color scheme remained true to Royston's design. The square was expanded to the southeast to include a large raised terrace with additional seating. Unfortunately, the site is now surrounded by higher buildings that block much of the sun, but this public space continues to be heavily used, attracting food carts on workdays and families on weekends.

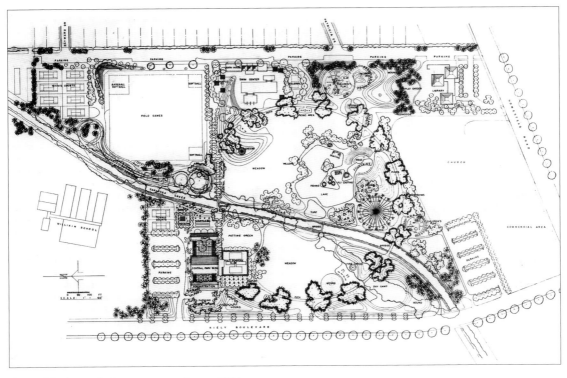

Central Park, preliminary master plan, c. 1961. RHAA.

CENTRAL PARK

SANTA CLARA, CALIFORNIA

1960–1975

Royston's success at Krusi and Mitchell Parks led to his design of Central Park in Santa Clara, a complicated and expensive project that would mark a turning point in his career. The commission came through Earl Carmichael, the city's director of parks and recreation, who also hired Royston to design several smaller neighborhood parks in a municipality that had quadrupled its population and doubled its land area in a mere decade. Over time, their shared vision of the potential of parks to create community spirit and encourage healthy recreation would develop into a personal friendship.[1]

Central Park was the first major project of Royston, Hanamoto & Mayes (RHM), the firm Royston established in 1958. The fifty-two-acre park included a public library, an international swim center with bleachers for over five thousand spectators, a baseball stadium, a children's zoo, and a tennis complex. The plan incorporated features that would become identified with Royston—the zoning of areas

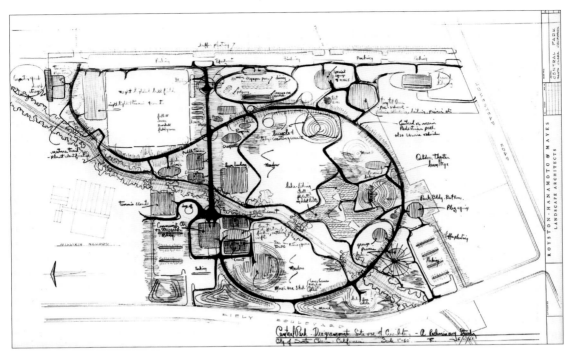

Site use and circulation preliminary study, 1961. RC EDA.

by function, well-defined spaces, a rich and varied planting plan, creative playgrounds, and the use of berms to shape the ground plane. At Central Park, RHM was given the space and freedom necessary to experiment with planting designs, spatial organization, and imaginative amenities for park users. Although Royston designed the original master plan in 1960, construction was phased in seventeen stages funded by a series of municipal bonds and not completed until the mid-1970s. During this period, partners Asa Hanamoto, David Mayes, Kazuo Abey, Louis Alley, and Harold Kobayashi provided substantial input on the design in keeping with the firm's team approach for complex projects.[2]

The city purchased the Central Park site, a former fruit

Aerial view, c. 1980. RHAA.

International swim center, c. 1975. JCM.

orchard, in 1959 at a cost of $700,000.[3] An irregular poly-
gon, the site was bordered on the west and south by major
thoroughfares. Saratoga Creek sliced across it from northeast
to southwest, creating a deep swale dividing the park into
two sections—the eastern portion approximately twice the
size of the western. An elementary school had recently been
built along the north boundary, and detached single-family houses surrounded the rest of the site. The first section
completed was east of Saratoga Creek, where Royston sited
the large public buildings and athletic facilities, using a sin-

gle access road to connect these features and accommodate curbside parking. By restricting automobiles to the park's eastern and southern edges, he allowed the majority of the park to remain a pedestrian area.

Royston defined the center of the park by creating a two-acre lake adjacent to its centerpiece—a monumental picnic pavilion bordered by two "meadow" areas on either side of Saratoga Creek. Curving pedestrian paths led out from the picnic structure, inviting exploration of the meadows. To provide structure and variety on the flat site, Royston shaped the earth into berms. The main path eventually circled back to its point of origin near the picnic pavilion, and along the way its branches connected to the numerous sports facilities on the eastern perimeter.

The circular picnic pavilion, the height of a seven-story building, rivaled the park's athletics facilities in scale. Resembling a festive circus tent, it was 160 feet in diameter, with a 75-foot-high steel column at its center from which a series of galvanized chains were suspended to form a canopy. Wisteria grew halfway up the chains, adding texture to the canopy and offering users a choice of sun or shade. The pavilion was circled by a raised terrace containing picnic tables, large barbecue grills, tables for food preparation, and sinks for cleanup. A landmark within the park, the pavilion proved so popular that a smaller version was developed for the west area of the park several years later.

The central two-acre lake, an irregular polygon articulated as a series of bays, became another space to be zoned for specific activities, such as fly-casting contests, model boating, and fishing. By dividing it into two levels, connected by a low waterfall (to aerate the water and produce a pleasant murmur), Royston created the type of multisensual experience characteristic of his work. Two large-scale spray

View across lake to picnic pavilion, c. 1965. JCM.

Fountain and picnic pavilion and wisteria-covered canopy, 2018. Photos by Tom Fitzgerald.

fountains and a tall jet supplied additional aeration, as well as visual interest, and cobblestones around the lake served as an aesthetically pleasing means of erosion control.

On the western side of Saratoga Creek, Royston used recycled materials in one of his most original playground designs. Large, cube-shaped granite blocks with hollow circular cores formed a series of climbing mazes. Royston discovered the raw materials, leftover hollowed-out blocks cut for the columns of San Francisco City Hall, when visiting a nearby quarry. After a sculptor added some rough texture to the blocks, Royston integrated them with swings and slides to form a playspace that continues to delight children.[4] The

Playground with recycled quarry blocks, c. 1975. JCM.

use of recycled materials for playground structures was rare at a time when most landscape architects were either designing their own play structures from new materials or ordering them from catalogs.

The western portion of the park also featured a unique amphitheater with wooden bench seating backed by an earthen berm and planted with a mixture of plants native to California. Unfortunately, this innovative method of showcasing the state's indigenous flora, reflecting an emerging ethic of environmentally oriented design, proved unrealistic. The foot traffic of children running up and down the slope obliterated the native planting before it could become well established.

Central Park's planting plan, one of Royston's most elaborate for a public project, used plants to help shape the visitor's experience. Hardy trees and shrubs, along with earthen berms, defined the different areas, and groves of redwoods anchored several corners of the park. Because the spaces were not completely walled off, visitors passing by caught glimpses of various activities, a safety precaution but also an invitation to join in. The views from inside the giant picnic pavilion exemplified this masterful orchestration of sight lines. From beneath the wisteria canopy, "windows" were created by support columns and the small trees ringing the space. One could see past the turf-covered berms to the lake and its large fountain jet. Majestic coast redwoods and bigleaf maples formed a distant backdrop enclosing the composition. As at Mitchell Park, the perimeters were not heavily buffered but kept clear to open up views deep into the interior. The two large meadows were left completely open, in contrast to the wall-like layering of trees on the central lawn of Mitchell Park, to better accommodate public events such as concerts and civic celebrations. During the

Presentation site model, c. 1960. JCM.

later phases of construction, Royston and his design team sited a community center (designed by the architect George Matsumoto) in the western portion of the park. The new center included facilities for the elderly and a playground for children with disabilities.

The park celebrated its official dedication in 1974 with a wide range of programs: a synchronized swimming and diving exhibition, sack races, a tennis exhibit, belly dancing, a baseball doubleheader, story time, a martial arts performance, and a safe-boating demonstration.[5] A similar variety of activities continues to the present day. Duck feeding has replaced fly-casting and the children's zoo was cut from the budget, but the facilities are little changed. The success of this complex park project reinforced Royston's reputation as an outstanding designer and helped his firm gain a range of commissions involving large-scale site planning, including campus plans, a new town, and additional parks in the Pacific Northwest.[6]

Stanford Linear Accelerator, aerial view of construction, 1962. Stanford Linear Accelerator Archives.

STANFORD LINEAR
ACCELERATOR CAMPUS

MENLO PARK, CALIFORNIA

1962–1963

Royston's design of a landscape for the "longest and straightest building of its kind in the world" exemplifies his willingness to take on utilitarian commissions related to the new building types and technologies of his generation.[1] The Klystron Gallery, a two-mile-long container for the country's first particle acceleration device, posed an interesting problem for a landscape architect accustomed to making spaces for people. During the year-long project, Royston demonstrated his characteristic ability to work collaboratively and to negotiate for his ideas, qualities that would also lead to the success and longevity of his firm. Even in a project as potentially bland as this landscape, he found a way to use his painterly eye to diminish the structure's form and create visual harmony from a distance.

Research into the use of high-frequency waves to accelerate electrons began on the Stanford campus in the 1930s. The first functioning particle acceleration device based on powerful new radio tubes called klystrons, the Klystron Mark I, occupied the cramped basement of the physics building. This technology, which would provide the basis for contemporary innovations such as magnetic resonance imaging (MRI), satellite communications, and telephone and television transmission, was rapidly developed during World War II for use in radar and aircraft navigation. Continued advances in the field during the postwar period garnered Stanford's particle physics and accelerator science programs international recognition, including a number of Nobel Prizes, and generated the need for new facilities to accommodate increasingly large structures.[2]

By the late 1950s, Stanford was planning a new venue for klystron-based research on a 480-acre site in the hills west of the main campus. The commission for the landscape came to Royston through Edward Ginzton, director during the research and development phase of the project, known at that time as "Project M" or "The Monster." In addition to directing research and obtaining funding, Ginzton led the staff committee that worked with a campus-based architectural advisory council to oversee the design of the new campus. Royston and Ginzton had met through the Ladera cooperative housing project, and when it failed to come to fruition, Royston designed gardens for the Ginzton home near the Ladera site in the hills above the Stanford campus.[3]

When RHMB was hired late in 1962, extensive planning had already been completed by Stanford's architectural and engineering teams. They focused on the equipment and materials required, but also prepared a detailed landscape master plan. With text and schematic graphics this plan described a central core for laboratory and administrative buildings, circulation for vehicles, large parking lots,

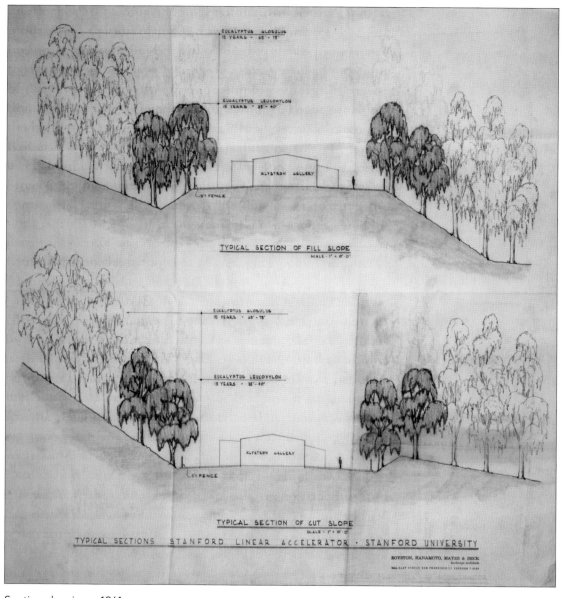

Section drawings, 1961. RC EDA.

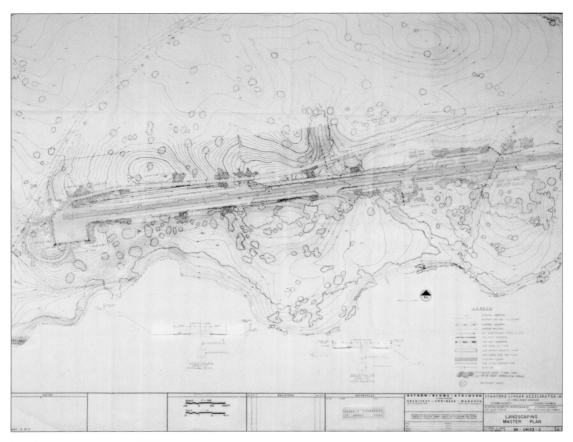

Landscape master plan, 1963. RC EDA.

storage areas, perimeter shop buildings, and maintenance facilities. The Klystron Gallery—nearly two miles long and only thirty feet wide—was to be continuous, open, and level from end to end. The landscape master plan described "belts of planting" surrounding "the outdoor storage and assembly spaces adjacent to the shops complex," to "screen the inevitable untidiness associated with physics shops and laboratories," and in addition made general suggestions for an incremental building schedule and recommended striving for "the greatest effect for the least cost."[4]

After reviewing Stanford's master plan for the site, RHMB prepared a landscape installation phasing plan and cost estimates and devised a strategy for obtaining an adequate supply of plants.[5] Royston and his office generally accepted the master plan developed for the SLAC core: a "close clipped lawn in the academic tradition with groves of shade trees providing pedestrians with some protection from sun, wind, and rain." The firm embellished this basic concept by adding a path system with meanders reminiscent of Royston's public park designs rather than a strictly parallel and perpendicular layout. Entrances to buildings were marked with handsome, modestly scaled plazas, and smaller patios shaded by trees were provided adjacent to the buildings, as recommended in the original master plan.

It was the challenge of the Klystron Gallery that drew Royston's attention and creative energies. In addition to the unusual proportions of the building, he confronted rigorous requirements for precision in the architecture, and the daunting task of siting a two-mile-long building. Extensive topographic surveys were prepared and a number of alternate positions studied to minimize grading and disturbance to the surrounding landscape, which would require repair and remediation after slopes were cut and filled. Royston also needed to consider the effects of the heat generated from the building's electrical equipment, an issue raised in Stanford's preliminary report, which proposed flanking the gallery on both sides with a nearly continuous line of deodar cedar to shade the structure from the sun.

In his initial comments on the plan Royston suggested a less formal approach to tree planting and offered a number of alternative species, noting that to provide effective shade, the planted trees should be medium to large size and eventually develop an arched branching pattern. He also observed that the gallery was oriented east to west, so that even the relatively low and small foliage canopy of young trees would shade the walls of the building in the early morning and later afternoon. Unlike his clients, Royston felt that the monotonous effect created by using a single species would call unwanted attention to the building. In his comments to the engineering committee and the architectural advisory council he suggested a number of pines and cedars, including beach pine, bishop pine, and incense cedar, a species native to California although not indigenous to the Stanford hills.[6] He expanded the tree list to include broadleaf evergreens, especially eucalyptus varieties, and suggested a more naturalistic planting strategy—breaking the line of trees at intervals and supplementing it with intermittent grove plantings. He proposed adding informal clusters of bluegum eucalyptus, especially in locations where slopes had been cut or filled. While these choices obviously had aesthetic implications, he explained the deviations from the master plan in terms of function and economy, justifying the groves as erosion control measures and pointing out that planting a large species such as bluegum on a slope would generate a visible effect more quickly.

Royston's understanding of the politics governing decision making in an academic environment proved helpful to him as he made his case. During the design development phase, extensive review of details large and small was made by both the Engineering Committee and the campus-based Architectural Advisory Council, which included the prominent Bay Area practitioners Gardner Dailey and Timothy Pflueger as well as Royston's mentor Thomas Church, the

Stanford campus landscape architect. Royston proved himself a skilled negotiator who was not only sensitive to the concerns of his client but also able to use his connection with Church to advance his own ideas, some of which ran contrary to the dictates of the original master plan. For example, during a meeting of the engineering staff committee, Royston recommended fieldstone as a wall material for the retaining walls required in many locations across the site rather than the committee's choice of concrete block.[7] To persuade his audience, Royston avoided aesthetic issues

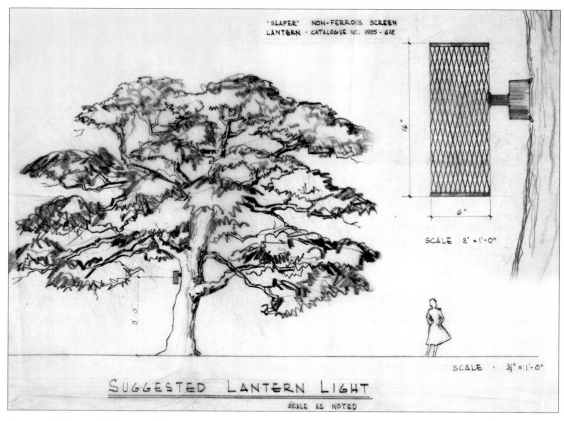

Lantern light study drawing, 1961. RC EDA.

View at night, 2011. Stanford Linear Accelerator Archives.

and couched his argument in terms of economy and function. He explained how stone could be placed by dry stacking, a technique that would be less labor intensive, more efficiently placed in curved layouts, and less expensive than block walls. Royston already knew Church would approve the choice, since he had used fieldstone walls liberally on the main campus.

The design for the Stanford Linear Accelerator project was both innovative and subtle. RHMB addressed a range of technical concerns while creating a subdued setting for a bizarre utilitarian structure in an otherwise pastoral landscape. For over a year, the firm worked with the Stanford team, helping the university develop an onsite nursery program to provide the nearly two thousand trees required and preparing a fencing plan to contain grazing cattle, the strategy for maintaining the grassland perimeter. The Klystron Gallery building, still in active use, remains an appropriate metaphor for the blend of native landscape and technical innovation characteristic of Silicon Valley.

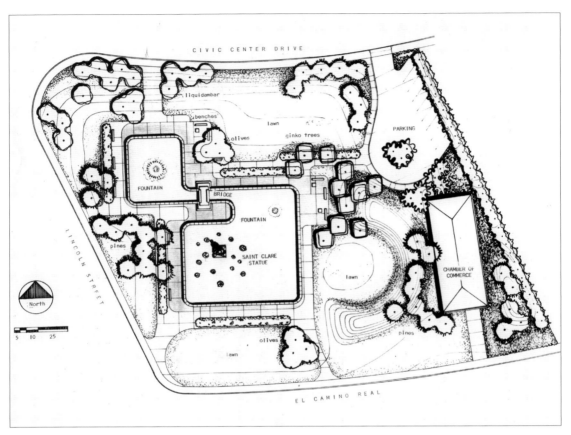

Santa Clara Civic Center Park, site plan, 1954. RC EDA.

SANTA CLARA
CIVIC CENTER PARK

SANTA CLARA, CALIFORNIA

1964

Royston was in the midst of work on Central Park when the Santa Clara parks and recreation director, Earl Carmichael, recommended him to design another new park for the city. Intended as a gateway to Santa Clara's $2 million civic center, the park was to be created on a three-acre parcel adjacent to Highway 82, the busy arterial El Camino Real, which followed the original eighteenth-century road connecting the Spanish missions. The awkward site was originally intended for a gas station, but just before construction began on the civic center, city planners purchased the property for a park. Royston faced the challenge of transforming this leftover piece of land into an accessible space with qualities to attract and delight.[1]

In its most basic form, Royston conceived of the park as an asymmetrical water parterre. Visitors entered from a parking lot at the northeast corner, adjacent to the chamber of commerce. The main path, bordered by planted "islands" on either side, led to two pools. A central, roughly rectangular pool with rounded corners was joined by a narrow strip of water to a second, smaller pool, which dominated the corner of the park farthest from the parking lot. The broad surfaces of the pools created a serene ambience, and their gracefully curving smooth raised edges added to the aura of sculptural refinement.[2] A spray fountain aerating the smaller pool to the north produced a soothing sound that helped diminish traffic noise.

The focal point of the composition was in the larger pool—a twenty-foot-high, three-ton bronze statue of St. Clare by Anne Van Kleeck hovering over the water on a seven-foot-high pedestal. The sculpture was chosen by the mayor's appointed statuary committee over twenty-four other submissions and approved by the city council despite the lobbying of some citizens who preferred a more realistic work. Although Royston was not involved in its selection, he skillfully sited the sculpture of Santa Clara's namesake, an early disciple of St. Francis of Assisi, in her nun's habit.[3] Placed off-center, the work introduced a slight spatial tension in an otherwise harmonious composition. Fourteen circular concrete planters of varying sizes, built into the pool and intended for flowers, were scattered about the statue to appear as if floating on the surface of the water. Linear flowerbeds near the pools added accents of color complementing those of the "floating" planters and provided a contrast with the predominantly green palette of the trees.[4] The pools were only one foot deep, a safety feature that also facilitated maintenance and conserved water. A second multiple-jet fountain in the far corner of the larger pool gently animated a small portion of its surface and formed a visual counterpoint to the statue.

To its east, a carefully sculpted semicircular turf berm

Aerial view, 1964. JCM.

backed by a wisteria fence served as a small amphitheater.
The park also provided a convenient and visible location
for the small chamber of commerce information building
sited on the city's eastern edge. Consulting with his colleagues Asa Hanamoto, David Mayes, and Eldon Beck,
Royston planted bosques of Italian stone pine, gingko, and

Annual planting, 1964. JCM.

American sweetgum to shade the many custom-designed benches. Over time, the pines surrounding the building contributed a backdrop to the amphitheater, and throughout the park the saplings Royston planted grew to be dense and defined space as he intended. Sweetgum, ginkgo, and olive trees edging the lawn on the north side of the main pool have also matured, creating a visually appealing, multicolored border.

Footbridge, 1964. JCM.

St. Clare statue, 2005. Photo by Reuben Rainey.

In this small urban park, Royston used high-quality materials, carefully chosen plants, and strong visual lines to create an urban oasis. A note of symbolism in his planting design complements that of the St. Clare statue. Clusters of olive trees were planted at each end of the site to recall expansive olive groves, once a mainstay of the regional economy.[5] Santa Clara Civic Center Park quickly became a local urban icon. St. Clare's statue, a landmark on El Camino Real, marked the entrance to the civic center, served as a backdrop for public events, and offered a welcoming presence in this unique public space.[6] The park, one of Royston's most elegant and well-conceived designs, is his best preserved work, having existed for almost a half century with only minor alterations to its planting plan.

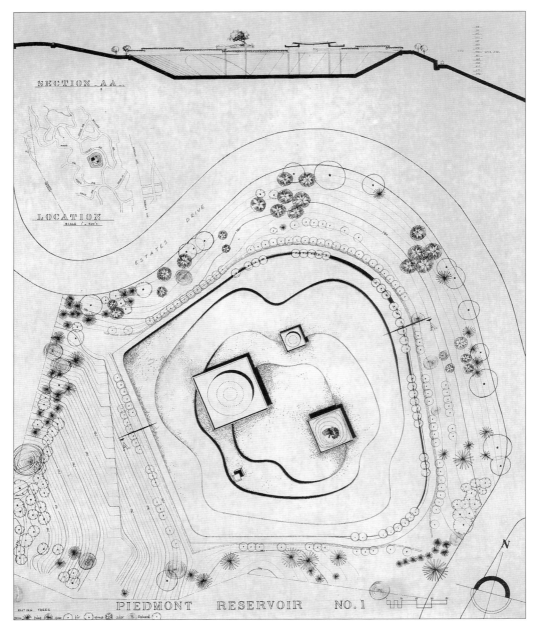

SECTION A.A.

LOCATION
SCALE 1" = 400's

ESTATES DRIVE

A

A

N

PIEDMONT RESERVOIR NO. 1

EXISTING TREES

Estates Reservoir, plan and section drawing, 1966. RC EDA.

ESTATES RESERVOIR

OAKLAND, CALIFORNIA

1968

In actualizing his "landscape matrix" concept, Royston took on a wide range of commissions but perhaps none as seemingly pedestrian as the designs for reservoir covers. During the 1960s, the East Bay Municipal Utilities District (EBMUD) hired RHA for a series of commissions involving reservoirs, filter plants, and pumping stations throughout the Bay Area. Rather than satisfying his client with utilitarian solutions, Royston treated the projects as components in a network. The cover he designed for a reservoir on a hilly eastern edge of San Francisco Bay not only sheltered the water supply but also became an artistic contribution to the surrounding landscape.

Unprecedented postwar population growth in the Bay Area generated a dramatic increase in demand for treated water in the region, and EBMUD recognized that its expanding infrastructure had become an integral, and often highly visible, part of the landscape. One aspect of the utility district's response to growth was the adoption of a "good neighbor" approach toward facilities design as a means of maintaining strong community relations.[1] This led to collaborations with design professionals beyond the engineering disciplines, including Robert Royston and his firm, Royston, Hanamoto, Mayes & Beck. Over a ten-year period ending with the completion of the Estates Reservoir cover in 1968, the office completed dozens of projects for EBMUD, including other covered reservoirs.

The Estates Reservoir, originally known as Piedmont No. 1, was initially constructed in 1903 by excavating a basin and constructing a fill dam on an existing seasonal stream. A concrete liner added in 1938 enlarged and strengthened the structure.[2] In the late 1950s, the East Bay Municipal Utilities District, the public agency that succeeded the privately held companies responsible for the first dam, began a systematic planning program for covering its treated water supplies. This work reflected a national postwar effort to cover reservoirs, motivated, at least in part, by Cold War–era concern about protecting urban water supplies from contamination.[3] Given that the majority of EBMUD's existing facilities were open reservoirs in residential districts, this project evolved into an extensive effort to retrofit the structures.

With the exception of his 1949 design for the Chinn garden in San Francisco, the Estates Reservoir roof covering was Royston's most explicit expression of landscape as abstract art. His aesthetic philosophy emphasized the visual arts, especially modern painting and sculpture, which rejected formal compositional strategies in favor of asymmetry and abstraction. Plan drawings of the reservoir cover suggest collage compositions by the modernist artist Jean Arp, whom Royston often cited as an inspiration. In a description of the project, Royston wrote that "the enhancement of the

Model, 1966. JCM.

fine view was desired as well as an element of beauty for the roof itself."[4]

Set in the center of a six-and-a-half-acre site, the reservoir cover was an irregular polygon with asymmetrically rounded corners, its longest dimension approximately three hundred feet across. The surface stepped down in a series of concentric biomorphic shapes punctuated by three square platforms set parallel to the face of the dam. Two of the platforms contained tall, jet-style fountains, and the third featured a mounded planter capped with a sculptural evergreen tree. The square platforms were cantilevered over their supporting bases, cre-

Aerial view, 1969. JCM.

ating a strong shadow line so that the platforms almost seemed to float. The platform edges were further embellished with a subtle arch pattern, a detail Royston described as a way to lead and reward the eye.[5] Royston emphasized the painterly composition of the design by specifying two colors of aggregate for the roof gravel—brown for the outer rings and tan in the center plane. Varied types and sizes of the aggregate were also used to create textural contrast from one plane to the next. The perimeter of the reservoir cover was defined by a low unadorned wall and a service path.

Royston's 1964 design for Santa Clara Civic Center Park anticipated his strategy for the reservoir cover project, in which landscape was primarily a visual experience. Public access to the reservoir was limited to views from the uphill sections of Estates Drive and nearby homes. In the RHMB design, the majority of existing trees ringing the site were retained and used to frame views of the reservoir and beyond to San Francisco Bay. An asymmetrical but rhythmic planting of large-scale groundcover shrubs reinforced the composition without detracting from the views. The reservoir

View across cover, 1969. JCM.

Street view, 2008. Photo by Charles Birnbaum.

cover also illustrates Royston's fascination with expressing temporal change and creating opportunities for sensory experiences. The sound of the fountains and the moving water captured the viewer's attention, while shifting shadow lines created by the edges of the elevated and overlapping roof planes altered the emphasis of the composition hourly and seasonally. The roof planes were not only aesthetically pleasing but also designed to ventilate the reservoir, a utilitarian detail Royston exploited to artistic advantage.

The RHMB design covered the Estates Reservoir for three decades with only minor alterations. In 2000, however, roof maintenance necessitated replacement of the original gravel aggregate, resulting in considerable loss of color and texture. Over time trees and vegetation grew into the framed view, further eroding the integrity of the design, and in 2008, in response to statewide water policies, regular operation of the fountains was discontinued. Finally, prompted by seismic safety concerns, EBMUD removed the roof covering and replaced the earthen dam with underground large-capacity storage tanks in 2011.[6]

Sunriver, master plan showing undeveloped northern section, 1967. RC EDA.

SUNRIVER

DESCHUTES COUNTY, OREGON

1968–1969

The commission for the recreation-based residential community of Sunriver finally enabled Royston to realize his ideal of a large-scale "landscape matrix." Twenty-four years after collaborating with Garrett Eckbo on Ladera, a residential community structured around a linear park, Royston created his ideal on the largest tract of land he had ever been commissioned to design—a five mile long, two mile wide, 5,500-acre parcel in Central Oregon. Royston, Hanamoto, Beck & Abey (RHBA) was selected to plan the landscape in collaboration with George T. Rockrise & Associates, a San Francisco–based architectural and planning firm responsible for the resort lodge and many of the residential units. Royston directed the site planning, receiving input from partners Asa Hanamoto, Kazuo Abey, and Patricia Carlisle, in keeping with the firm's team approach. The first phase of the development opened in June 1968.[1]

Sunriver's developers, Donald V. McCallum and John D.

Gray, envisioned "a new community carefully planned to preserve a harmonious balance between man and nature." Over a twenty-year period, the recreational resort was to develop into a new town with schools, churches, a venue for nonpolluting manufacture, research facilities, and year-round residences as well as vacation homes. All measures would be taken "to preserve the natural beauty . . . and keep the air, land, and waterways fresh and unspoiled." The developers' long-term plan was for a community of twelve to fifteen thousand residents.[2]

Lagoon bridge, 1990. Photo by Royston. JCM.

Located on the eastern slope of the Cascade Range, a day's drive from most of Oregon's major urban areas, the site was remote enough to provide a sense of respite from city life. An eight-mile stretch of the meandering Deschutes River, one of the nation's premier trout streams, defined the site's western border, and the property was enclosed on its other three sides by the Deschutes National Forest, a protective barrier against future development. Forests of ponderosa pine, lodgepole pine, and Engelmann spruce covered much of the gently rolling terrain dotted with lava outcroppings. The site was not pristine, however. During World War II, a small portion of it functioned as Camp Abbot, a training facility for army engineers to practice building combat environments, such as artillery emplacements and tank traps. The camp was decommissioned in 1944 and completely demolished except for its airstrip and officers' club. The design for Sunriver incorporated these elements, lengthening the airstrip to accommodate small jets, and renovating the officers' club as a restaurant and wedding banquet venue. The town of Bend, fifteen miles to the north, offered medical facilities and an abundance of restaurants and shops.[3]

The initial program for Sunriver called for a lodge with over two hundred rooms, a swimming pool, a large playground, and restaurants. Housing was arranged in sixteen clusters of eight to fifteen lots, ranging in size from one-eighth to one-half acre, which were then grouped into seven neighborhoods served by loop roads and cul-de-sacs to prevent through-traffic. Housing types varied from two-story condominiums to privately owned detached houses. Over the twenty-year projected growth period, a total of five to six thousand dwelling units were planned, along with two championship golf courses, an additional aquatic

Main lodge with foothills of Cascades in distance, 1990.
Photo by Royston. JCM.

Deck at main lodge, 1990.
Photo by Royston. JCM.

Cabin-style housing, 1985.
Photo by Kenneth Helphand.

Condominiums, 1985. Photo by
Kenneth Helphand.

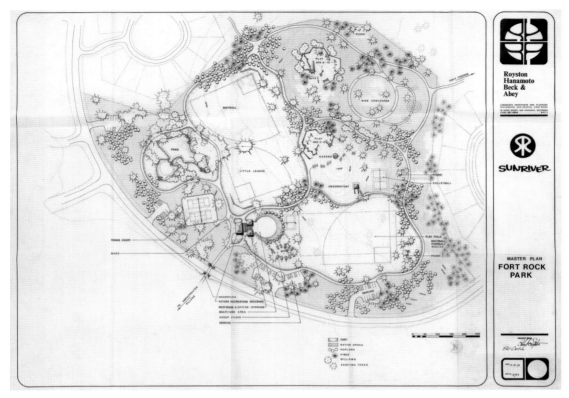

Fort Rock Park master plan, c. 1968–70. RC EDA.

center, a tennis facility, a nature study center with resident ecologist, a marina, equestrian stables, two parks, and a shopping mall.[4]

The entire eight-mile riverfront was preserved for hiking and boating, and a two-mile still-water lagoon with small islands was constructed near the lodge to provide additional boating and hazards for one of the golf courses. A bird sanctuary was located midway along the riverfront. A large six-hundred-acre "Great Meadow" formed the heart of the community. Located near the lodge and bisected by the fenced airstrip, this central space was left in grassland

Riverfront preservation area, 1990. Photo by Royston. JCM.

The "Great Meadow," 1969. JCM.

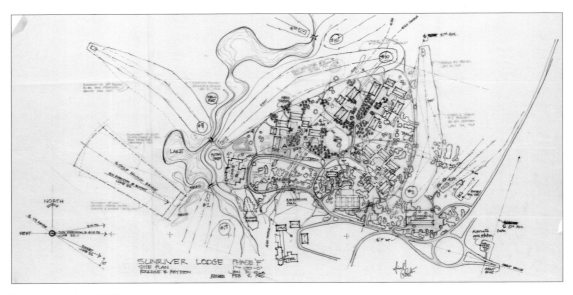

Lodge site plan, 1968. RC EDA.

as a grazing area for cattle and horses. It formed a pastoral foreground for views of the mountains to be enjoyed from the verandas of the lodge.[5]

Royston tied together this array of spaces for housing and recreation with a landscape matrix connecting various distinct components of the site. The automobile road system was entirely separate from a twenty-five-mile network of paths for walking, bicycling, and driving electric golf carts. This path system connected residential areas and recreational facilities more directly than the roads, which were minimized as much as possible. Paved with a mixture of asphalt and fine-grained gravel, these twelve-foot-wide paths were buffered on either side by greenways or "linear parklike" areas that Royston called the "primary nature reserves." The residential lot clusters forming the "villages" were also separated from one another by preserving the "secondary nature reserves" between them.

Path, 1990. Photo by Royston. JCM.

Commercial area, 1990. Photo by Royston. JCM.

Road and bike trail separation, 1985. Photo by Kenneth Helphand.

The spaces between individual house lots were designated as "common natural areas," with strict regulations limiting removal of vegetation. Royston planted the main and secondary road systems with thick walls of trees on both sides to separate them from the villages and to reduce noise. When a pedestrian path crossed a major road, it was often via an underpass. This network of buffered paths and roads furnished ready access to all the other greenspaces, including the two small parks, the Great Meadow, the lagoon, the riverfront, and the bird sanctuary.[6]

Although Royston planned his matrix for the entire five-by-two-mile site, only the southern portion, about half the area, was actually constructed. Sunriver failed to expand at the expected rate—the northern portion still awaits development—but the successful resort has a year-round population of about seventeen hundred. The only extensive realization of Royston's landscape matrix, Sunriver's pedestrian-oriented circulation system and integrated series of parks and nature reserves is a model for designers seeking to create more ecologically planned neighborhoods and towns.[7]

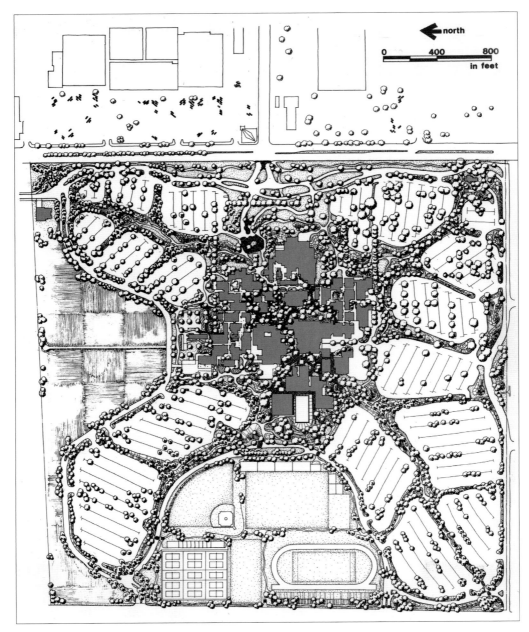

San Joaquin Delta College, site plan and context drawing, 1969. RC EDA.

SAN JOAQUIN
DELTA COLLEGE

STOCKTON, CALIFORNIA

1969–1978

Royston was engaged in a range of projects for institutions of higher education throughout his career. Commissions varied in scale and complexity from simple planting plans to designs for entire new campuses, especially for the community colleges proliferating in California in the 1960s.[1] The rapid growth of these two-year colleges was fueled by the state legislature's passage of the Donahue Act of 1960, which called for the development of the largest tuition-free community college system in the nation.[2] The influx of community college campus commissions presented unique and ongoing opportunities for Royston to experiment with the landscape matrix and to implement its environmentally sound planning principles.

A generation later, RHAA published a promotional brochure summarizing its design methodology for this project type: "Knowledgeable and well-directed campus planning . . . can lead to what we hope to achieve in many cities—

total pedestrian precincts in which people can live and work free from the noise and pollution of the automobile and where the integration of landscape and architecture is synthesized."[3] In its collaboration with the architectural firms Ernest J. Kump Associates and Gwathmey, Sellier, Crosby on the design of San Joaquin Delta College, RHBA would realize many aspects of its ideal landscape matrix. Eldon Beck led the RHBA design team that included Kazuo Abey and Harold Kobayashi.[4] Hiko Takada of Kump Associates was the primary design architect.

The original vision for San Joaquin Delta College, a new two-year commuter college, came from its board of trustees. In fall 1968, the board decided to break from the traditional approach of housing academic disciplines in separate buildings and instead divide the college into five "instructional centers," each with "a central open courtyard, snack bar, and study lounge" in addition to classrooms. One center offers courses in agriculture, natural resources, broadcasting, visual arts, early childhood education, business, and photography. Another combines physical education, life science, public safety and services, computer science, and printing. A third includes classes in music, machine technology, heating and air conditioning, welding, and engineering. Another offers instruction in nursing, business, and drama. The fifth houses vocational shops, physical education, athletics, and dance facilities. The blending of disparate disciplines reflects the trustees' egalitarian philosophy and desire that "students with greatly different backgrounds and career interests—from musicians to mechanics—meet in hallways, lounges, and classrooms, and learn to respect each other's values."[5] Kump's firm used a three-by-three-meter grid to site the five centers as well as the library, gym, and administration building. Buildings and their small courtyards were staggered in an asymmetrical pattern,

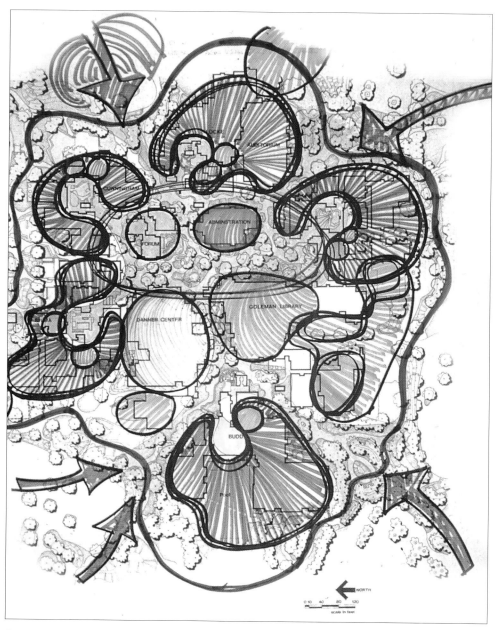

Campus core study diagram prepared by Eldon Beck, 1969. RC EDA.

Small courtyard, 2018. Photo by JC Miller.

avoiding the bilateral symmetry characteristic of many American campus plans.

The college's 165-acre site was located in the California Delta region, known as "The Holland of California." Formed by the confluence of the Sacramento and San Joaquin Rivers, the delta contains some of the richest agricultural land in the state, drained by an elaborate system of levees and dikes.

The Stockton State Hospital was previously located on the site, and its farm was worked by patients as therapy and to provide food for the institution. When the hospital closed in the mid-1960s, the agricultural fields became available for the college. The site contained numerous mature trees that Beck's team was careful to preserve. Since the terrain was relatively flat in a region prone to flooding, the drainage of the parcel required careful attention.[6]

In collaboration with the two architectural firms, RHBA responded to the trustees' educational aims and to the site by clustering the college buildings and courtyards in a central pedestrian precinct. Automobiles were accom-

Aerial view of campus showing wildflowers in perimeter parking areas, 1972. Eldon Beck Collection, EDA.

Perimeter path, 2018. Photo by JC Miller.

modated by fifteen parking lots on the campus perimeter. The central pedestrian campus was accessed by means of a series of pathways elevated on berms intended to echo the dikes characteristic of the landscape. A busy ring road circled the outer perimeter of the parking lots and curved inward on the north and east edges of the site to allow for future expansion and create space for the college's athletic facilities: a baseball diamond, track, tennis courts, and football field.[7]

This design, with its emphasis on pedestrian access, was elegant and functional but not new. In 1960, Kump & Associates, working with the landscape architectural firm Sasaki, Walker & Associates, had designed such a plan for Foothill College in Los Altos Hills. Four years later, while collaborating on a similar plan for De Anza College in Cupertino, Beck and Kump recognized the value of designing the campus to exclude automobiles from its academic center. At San Joaquin Delta, Beck and his team

Parking lot with shade trees and perimeter berms, 2018. Photo by JC Miller.

adapted the Kump plan to the particular context and environmental needs of the site. RHBA began by excavating the parking lots below grade so they could function as stormwater retention basins to handle intermittent flooding. The parking lots were subdivided by rows of trees and slanted to align with the pedestrian berms that formed radial connections to the academic buildings. The edges of the lots were delineated as gradually meandering curves to blend them with the surrounding landscape in a treatment consistent with the topography of the delta region.[8]

The berms, which converged on the central pedestrian precinct at its four corners, were heavily planted with trees to provide shade in the hot summers. They featured unmowed banks of native bunch grasses and perennial wildflowers, a naturalistic planting design that gracefully transitioned into a more formal or "urban" planting scheme within the central academic building cluster. This use of a native plant palette on such a large scale and in such a highly visible location reflected the increasing sensitivity to environmental issues taking shape in the Royston office.[9] Earthen berms in the central area were planted with turf, and a small, two-level pond with curvilinear brick edges was featured in one of the smaller plazas. All of the buildings were slightly raised on berms to facilitate drainage, a challenge on the relatively flat site. Pedestrian paths led to a central "tree court" bordered by the library, administration building, student union, and two of the instructional centers. This central piazza-like space was heavily planted with trees, as were the surrounding walks and plazas. Trees were a mixture of hardy deciduous and evergreen species such as Chinese elm, Raywood ash, eucalyptus, Afghan pine, and stone pine.

Since the opening of the college's first academic center

Central quad pond and waterfall, 2018. Photo by JC Miller.

in 1973, several buildings have been added—including an art gallery, a theater complex, and a horticulture center—none of which has compromised the integrity of the original design. The campus layout, with its skillful separation of vehicular and pedestrian spaces—an academic center elevated above circumferential parking lots—is often referred to as "an acropolis plan," an oblique reference to the plan of ancient Athens, with its hilltop sacred precinct.

Community college commissions declined sharply in the 1970s. RHBA's last major project involving the cre-

Campus core path, 2018. Photo by JC Miller.

Fountain terrace, 2018. Photo by JC Miller.

ation of an entirely new campus was a 1970 collaboration
with the St. Louis architectural firm of Murphy, Downey,
Wofford & Richman on the site plan for Sangamon State
University near Springfield, Illinois. This plan repeated
the now-familiar template of a pedestrian core ringed by
parking lots.[10] Most of RHBA's subsequent work for educational institutions involved smaller-scale site plans for new
university buildings, such as UC San Francisco's School
of Dentistry (1980) and UC Berkeley's Engineering Building (1983). Although it was no longer engaged in creating entirely new campus plans, RHBA and its successor,

Holt courtyard steps, 2018.
Photo by JC Miller.

Students in Holt courtyard, 1972. Eldon Beck Collection, EDA.

RHAA, continued to emphasize the design principles and values embodied in the San Joaquin Delta College plan: the landscape matrix, with its focus on pedestrian environments and connected outdoor spaces fostering social interaction and responsible stewardship of the environment.

Veterans Administration   **Master Plan**
National Cemetery
Riverside California

Riverside National Cemetery, master plan, 1976. Courtesy Louis Alley.

RIVERSIDE NATIONAL CEMETERY

RIVERSIDE, CALIFORNIA

1976–1978

In its first venture into cemetery design, RHBA created a prototype for national military cemeteries near Riverside. The firm's choice of site and design response is a clear indication of its growing emphasis on sustainability and environmental stewardship, as well as its increasing ability to take on larger, more complex commissions. The project for Riverside National Cemetery offers a window into the inner workings of RHBA, illustrating the success of the collaborative approach Robert Royston incorporated into the structure of his firm.[1]

Initially, RHBA was commissioned only to select the site for a massive new veterans cemetery in Southern California. In 1975, the firm recommended acquiring part of the March Air Force Base, a site within a hundred-mile radius of half the population of California and near a reliable source of wastewater for irrigation. President Ford's Commission for National Cemeteries and Monuments formally designated 750 acres of the base for the new cemetery in 1976. The government's approval of RHBA's plan to reuse a military property and recycle water reflects a growing concern with environmental issues. Principal Louis G. Alley, who served as design team leader, later commented on how this choice influenced the design of the cemetery, noting that had the commission been offered a decade earlier, the Veterans Administration would have purchased a pristine site.[2] After helping determine the location, RHBA competed with other firms for the design commission. Alley's presentation included images of water features, sculpted turf, and structures in Royston's popular Bay Area parks.[3] The VA design committee's respect for this work won the firm the commission.

Royston was not an official member of the team, but he helped set the tone for the project by offering his suggestions in the early conceptual design phase. In addition to Louis Alley, the team was composed of principals Asa Hanamoto, Patricia Carlisle, and Kazuo Abbey. Throughout the design process, they worked closely with the National Cemetery Administration's newly appointed design committee to oversee this particular project and also collaborated with the architectural firm Leland King & Associates of Menlo Park. The team embarked on a six-phase development plan, using landforms and tree massing to symbolize the "dignity of burial and respect of memory."[4] Phase one, consisting of ninety-five acres, was completed and opened for burials in November 1978. To enhance the dignified, parklike ambience, rectangular twelve-by-twenty-four-inch grave markers were placed flush with the ground plane and situated in large, sweeping, meadow-like areas of closely mown turf. Although the chosen aesthetic resembled that of the early twentieth-century "memorial park cemeteries" pioneered

Meadow graves with columbarium complex in distance, 2016. Photo by JC Miller.

by Forest Lawn in Glendale, California, RHBA's initial plan did not include the figurative sculpture typical of such early designs.[5]

Despite the benefits that led RHBA to choose the Riverside location, the noisy, flat site presented many challenges. The designers planned a six-foot-high stone-clad wall to reduce traffic noise from Interstate 215 on the site's east border and Van Buren Boulevard, a major arterial along the north edge. Behind the wall, RHBA used concrete blocks left on the site as fill to create a series of earthen berms, planting their summits with clusters of evergreens. This treatment contributed to the sense of the cemetery as a realm set apart from the hectic world. Berms were also used to create overlooks in the southwest, center, and northeast areas of the site, and as barriers on its south and west borders. An eighteen-hole golf course abutting the west border and vacant land owned by the base to the south served as a partial buffer.

The plan reflected RHBA's belief that "modern cemetery design" should combine "the traditional elements of formality and order with freer forms and less structured spaces."[6] The formal element, a dual carriageway divided by a fifteen-foot median strip, ran the length of the cemetery,

Main entry drive and gate, 1978. Photo by Louis Alley.

Lake at entry and administration building, 1978. Photo by Louis Alley.

following the alignment of the remnants of a two-lane road on the former army training site. The monumental boulevard was punctuated by three equally spaced traffic circles named for World War II leaders General Dwight D. Eisenhower, Fleet Commander Chester W. Nimitz, and General James Harold "Jimmy" Doolittle and intended for burial sites or monuments.

RHBA's design choreographed the visitor's experience, beginning at the main entrance on Van Buren Boulevard. After passing through an elegant steel gate flanked by eight-foot stone-clad concrete walls, the visitor senses the presence of two ten-foot-high earthen berms behind the walls, forming a threshold into the consecrated landscape. The formal boulevard curves gracefully to the left, passing by the administration building and then continuing alongside a lake and a flag plaza before curving right and becoming the long, straight north–south axis. A section of the boulevard near the administration building is widened to allow the assembly of funeral processions, which follow a system of eight twelve-foot-wide curvilinear roadways branching off the main avenues, leading to the various burial areas. These more informal areas of gently curving roads and lush, undulating meadows are the setting for the bronze and granite grave markers in the memorial section of the cemetery. The markers are barely visible from the roadway, so the landscape resembles a vast green urban park, an oasis in its arid surroundings.

RHBA chose the locations for the maintenance cen-

Interment ceremony shelter, 1978. Photo by Louis Alley.

Interment ceremony shelter with amphitheater on opposite shore, 2016. Photo by JC Miller.

ter, administration building, and committal service shelters designed by King & Associates. The shelters are dispersed throughout the site to maintain the parklike ambiance. Louis Alley designed the cemetery's three columbaria in keeping with the style of the architecture and stone-clad perimeter walls. RHBA chose gray concrete for section indicators and backless benches, which had seats embedded with a mosaic of blue tiles.

Although four lakes were proposed for the site, as a means of storing irrigation water and reinforcing the parklike atmosphere, only two have been constructed in the first four phases. They are each divided into two levels connected by a small waterfall, a design seen in earlier RHBA parks. The elevation change between the sections facilitates the flow of water in the irrigation system. The lakes are also animated with spray fountains similar to those in Royston's Santa Clara Central Park. A large amphitheater, designed by the RHBA team for programmed events, is located on the shoreline of the phase one southern lake, providing a panoramic view across the water to the meadows and columbaria beyond.

Shade structures at amphitheater, 2016. Photo by JC Miller.

Terraced burial areas, 2016. Photo by JC Miller.

Columbarium with bell tower, 2016. Photo by JC Miller.

The planting plan, developed for the arid regional climate, centered around hardy evergreens, such as Afghan and stone pine. These were interspersed with London plane and various species of eucalyptus to form the groves framing the meadows. To emphasize the long views across the meadows and simplify maintenance, no understory shrubs were planted in the groves and the columbaria contained no foundation planting. Forty Mexican fan palms, donated by a local landowner, were later used to mark important features of the site, including the amphitheater, visitor center, columbaria, and committal service shelters.[7] Eucalyptus trees were added to those surviving along the old roadway to form a tree canopy over the new wide boulevard. Clusters of smooth, large boulders are embedded along the lakeshore and the edges of the interment service shelters.

Despite some changes, Riverside National Cemetery retains its original aesthetic character. In 1999, a Medal of Honor Memorial was located at Nimitz Circle, terminating the central boulevard, and over the next five years two additional monuments with figurative sculpture were built near the main entrance. Today phase four is partially completed, with 276 acres constructed and total number of graves more than 228,000; Riverside is the third-largest and most active of the 135 cemeteries managed by the National Cemetery Administration.[8] This significant memorial landscape led to RHBA's development of six other military cemeteries in the United States as well as veterans cemeteries in Santiago, Chile, and Kuala Lumpur, Malaysia.

Harris garden, model, 2008. Photo by Jennifer Loring. JCM.

HARRIS GARDEN

PALM SPRINGS, CALIFORNIA

2007

In 2007, Royston began what was to be his final design project, the Harris garden, in Palm Springs. The culmination
of a decades-long professional practice, the Harris garden
employs many of his most successful design principles and
includes signature forms and techniques applied to a unique
site in a challenging climate. The project began with a telephone call from the homeowner, Brent Harris, to JC Miller,
at that time a principal at Royston, Hanamoto, Alley &
Abey. Harris inquired whether Royston would be interested
in taking on a residential commission. When asked about
it, Royston winked and quipped that he "might" be able to
work it into his schedule.[1] Both forward-thinking and retrospective, this garden expands our understanding of Royston's
remarkable contribution to the field of landscape design.

The Harris garden is located on a two-parcel, approximately one-acre site that slopes gently from south to north.
The neighborhood was developed early in the history of

Palm Springs very close to the base of Mount San Jacinto, the highest escarpment in the continental United States. The mountain rises abruptly from the desert floor to the west of the city, generating a long period of extended twilight each evening. The property comprises two architecturally significant modern homes, on the northern end a house designed by Welton Becket & Associates in 1957 and a larger structure on the southern end, known as the Hefferlin house (after the couple who built it in 1961), designed by Richard George Wheeler with additions by Albert Frey. Both homes were completely renovated by the Harrises, who restored the Becket house to an original footprint. All work was guided by Brad Dunning.

On his first visit to Palm Springs, Royston was fascinated by the site and its unfamiliar desert context. Standing at the edge of the property on a sunny afternoon in May 2007, he looked west toward the dramatically steep, rock-strewn slope of Mount San Jacinto and observed, "The houses ought to be surrounded by authentic desert. Let's bring the scales" (his term for the large flat overlapped stones that characterize the mountainside) "right down to the house."

While walking the property with Harris, Royston noted that most of the neighborhood gardens were enclosed with block walls, metal picket fences, and high hedges that strictly followed property lines. Although he accepted the need for privacy and security, he proposed a more gracious arrangement of walls and hedges to keep the house from looking "like a fortress." Royston strongly believed that every garden should be at least partially visible when approached, "a gift to the street." For the entry to the circular Hefferlin house, he designed dramatic circular walls and gates which provided a glimpse inside while creating privacy.

When he returned to his home studio in Mill Valley,

Hefferlin house, entry, 2019. Photo by Millicent Harvey.

Harris garden model: detail of Hefferlin house pool garden, 2008. Photo by Jennifer Loring.

Royston set about developing a suite of gardens that would complement the two architecturally distinct houses. As he had seventy years earlier for his own and his neighbor Joseph Stein's properties, in Palm Springs Royston addressed the various garden spaces as elements in a single design. While each landscape passage has a distinct character and responds to the adjacent architecture, there is a unity to the plan that is unusual for the neighborhood. For the Harris garden, he proposed subdividing zones into areas for specific uses, a series of spaces that included a perimeter landscape at the street frontages, controlled entry spaces with driveways through the carports, expansive pool decks and lawns for private enjoyment in the protected back gardens, and small private patios adjacent to bedrooms.

His unified approach to the landscape designs of the two houses is first apparent at the shared street frontage. Here Royston proposed a curved planter in front of the Becket house to introduce and offset the strong circular privacy walls at the Hefferlin house. These "contrary" curves, as he called them, were a favorite device used to add energy and tension to his designs.

Although he did not prepare detailed plans or planting specifications for the project, Royston provided specific instructions that included his thoughts on texture and character for the planting in each of the garden areas. As had been his practice with other important commissions throughout his career, Royston insisted that a model be made to represent his design concept in three dimensions. Following Royston's guidance, Miller and his RHAA colleagues developed the construction plan and planting design.

For the desert perimeter Royston called for gray or muted green foliage and a limited flower color palette of yellow and white—hues appropriate to his idea of "authentic desert." To accomplish Royston's vision, more than two hundred tons of stone closely matching local geology were placed at the perimeter of the properties and populated with plants native to the region.

Inside this outermost zone, Royston envisioned an area of transition from the public street to the privacy of the home. This zone would be more densely planted with appropriate though not necessarily native desert species. Where possible, existing mature plants were retained and pruned to emphasize their sculptural qualities. The third, interior zone, which he called "the oasis," included a swimming pool, a spa, and patios for al fresco dining and sunbathing as well as protected spaces at the back and sides of each house. The oasis featured a broader palette of flowering plants and the only turf lawns on the property.

The radial floor plan of the Hefferlin house dictated the form of the largest of the private spaces in its oasis zone. When visiting the site, Royston noted the alignment of the interior walls and how the angles would "control the view out from each of these rooms" by directing "the eye to the center." He responded to the architecture with a radial, concentric garden focused on a large central pool. When

Hefferlin house, pool garden, 2013. JCM.

Hefferlin house, interior view to pool, 2016. Photo by Brent R. Harris.

discussing his plan, Royston cited as inspiration Wassily Kandinsky's painting *Several Circles* (1926).[2] Following this pattern, he added the circular forms of a fountain with a waterfall to enliven the surface of the pool, curbed planting areas, low garden tables, and planters in an asymmetrical arrangement. He also proposed large circular floats for the pool, which he called "lily pads," to add movement to the composition, but they were not included in the finished garden.

As part of the architectural remodel of the Hefferlin house, a block wall had been built to screen the back of the garage from view. For further spatial definition of the

Hefferlin house, pool garden, 2019. Photo by Millicent Harvey.

Hefferlin house garden, view to mountains, 2019. Photo by Brent R. Harris.

pool garden, Royston added a curved bench that effectively completed the circular space around the pool. The resulting space responds to the concave slopes of Mount San Jacinto which form the dramatic backdrop to the garden. Behind the wall he added a raised planter bed and a curved walkway with an elevated spot for a bench, creating a quiet and more intimately scaled place to sit and look down into the garden. Three tall Mexican fan palms were relocated from another part of the garden to provide a vertical counterpoint to the flat planes of turf, concrete paving, and water.

Becket guesthouse garden, biomorphic lawn panels, 2017. Photo by Brent R. Harris.

In the large open garden that Royston imagined for the oasis zone of the Becket house, the eastern section is devoted to a concrete terrace with a lap pool, the remainder to turf panels and a perimeter planting of citrus trees and flowering hedges. One of the lawn panels, intended as a putting green, was depressed six inches to create a boundary curb to help contain golf balls. Royston raised the lap pool above the level of the adjacent pool deck to seat height. Envisioning the terrace as a place for parties, he was looking to provide informal seating for anticipated activities. (One of his preliminary sketches includes the note "dancing?") For the back garden at the Becket house, Royston, with characteristic attention to how people interact with the landscape, arranged his vertical picket screens to shield the outdoor shower and a utility area from view and used a semicircular screen to define and enclose a seating area. (He had first used the screen in his 1949 design for the Standard Oil Rod & Gun Club in Point Richmond, as a structural approach to controlling breezes.)

Royston created a seamless transition between the two properties with the terrace adjacent to the Hefferlin house sunroom, negotiating an eighteen-inch difference in elevation. When the homes were first built, a retaining wall topped with a block privacy wall marked the boundary and managed the grade change between parcels. Royston proposed removing a sixteen-foot-wide section of the wall and extending the sunroom terrace north across the property line, terminating in wide, shallow stairs that negotiated the change in elevation. This stair configuration allows movement up and down at an angle, which he believed to be a natural and comfortable direction of travel. The connection between the previously separate properties is subtle but critically important to the flow between them.

The sunroom, a part of the addition to the Hefferlin

Hefferlin house, sunroom terrace, 2019. Photo by Millicent Harvey.

house designed by Albert Frey, features walls of glass and sliding-glass doors. Royston took advantage of this transparent corner of the house to create a strong, direct connection to the garden. The adjoining terrace is furnished with a garden pavilion original to the property (relocated from the pool garden), an in-ground spa, circular garden tables, and planters set close to the ground for dramatic effect. From here, one can move south into the pool garden, north to the Becket back garden, or east to private patios of bedrooms in the Frey addition. Anticipating the need to separate the gardens at times, he called for a rolling gate matching the height of the adjacent block wall.

The Harris garden commission came to Royston late in his life. During the weekly design meetings, he occasionally joked about his declining health: "I've only got two things going on right now—appointments with doctors and this garden." An unwavering optimist, he never acknowledged that this might be his last garden, and yet he seemed to perceive it as the likely culmination of his professional experience. He brought a lifetime of insight to the Harris garden and, having the freedom to incorporate past successes, he created a place that reflected his design philosophy but also embraced the future. In a fitting conclusion to his life's work, Royston deftly adapted his ideas to the contemporary needs of his client. The result is a garden that is truly timeless.

CHRONOLOGY OF
THE ROYSTON FIRM

1940–1941: Royston worked in the office of Thomas Church

1945–1958: Eckbo, Royston & Williams (ERW)
PARTNERS
Garret Eckbo
Robert Royston
Edward Williams

1958–1960: Royston, Hanamoto & Mayes (RHM)
PRINCIPAL OWNERS★
Robert Royston
Asa Hanamoto
David R. Mayes

1960–1966: Royston, Hanamoto, Mayes & Beck (RHMB)
PRINCIPAL OWNERS
Robert Royston
Asa Hanamoto
David R. Mayes
Eldon Beck

1967–1979: Royston, Hanamoto, Beck & Abey (RHBA)
PRINCIPAL OWNERS
Robert Royston
Asa Hanamoto
Eldon Beck
Kazuo Abey

PRINCIPAL
Patricia A. Carlisle

1978: Office relocates from San Francisco to Mill Valley

1979: Royston, Hanamoto, Alley & Abey (RHAA)
PRINCIPAL OWNERS
Robert Royston
Asa Hanamoto
Louis G. Alley
Kazuo Abey
Patricia A. Carlisle
Harold Kobayashi

PRINCIPAL
George Garvin

1989–2008: Royston, Hanamoto, Alley & Abey transition to RHAA
PARTNER/OWNERS
Harold Kobayashi
Cordelia Hill
Manuela King
Barbara Lundburg
William Fee
Aditya Advani

PRINCIPALS
Craig Hanchett
James Ingels
JC Miller
Doug Nelson
Jimmy Chan
Nathan Lozier

2009–Present: RHAA

PARTNER/OWNERS
Jimmy Chan
Manuela King
Nathan Lozier
Barbara Lundburg
Douglas Nelson

PRINCIPAL
James Ingels

★Before the transition period, partners (individuals with ownership in the firm) were referred to as Principal Owners. Patricia Carlisle was a Royston, Hanamoto, Beck & Abey Principal but not a partner until the formation of Royston, Hanamoto, Alley & Abey. George Garvin was a Royston, Hanamoto, Alley & Abey Principal but not a partner.

Beginning in the transition period and continuing to the present, the firm uses a two-tier leadership structure of Partner/Owners and Principals with management responsibility but no ownership stake.

The original partner group retired individually between 1989 and 1995. Robert Royston retired in 1989 but continued to consult on specific projects until his death in 2008. Several of the other retired partners also continued in consulting roles as Emeritus Partners.

NOTES

OVERVIEW

1. These interviews were conducted on July 8 and 9, 2002, in Mitchell, Bowden, Cuesta, Bowers, and Millbrae Parks, all located on the San Francisco Peninsula.

2. *A Community Park* is available on the Internet Archive at https://archive.org/details/VTS011_20190129.

3. See RHAA website, www.rhaa.com/index.php/practice/philosophy.

4. For details of Royston's early life, see Reuben M. Rainey and JC Miller, *Modern Public Gardens: Robert Royston and the Suburban Park* (San Francisco: William Stout, 2006), chap. 1.

5. Interview by authors, January 26, 2003.

6. Ibid.

7. Royston, "A Landscape Architect Considers Change in Practices Since His Church Apprenticeship," in *Thomas Dolliver Church, Landscape Architect,* 2 vols., interviews conducted by Suzanne B. Riess, Regional Oral History Office, Bancroft Library, University of California, Berkeley, 1978 (Royston interview, March 11, 1976), 1:214.

8. Michael Laurie, with David Streatfield, *75 Years of Landscape Architecture at Berkeley: An Informal History, Part I: The First 50 Years* (Berkeley: Department of Landscape Architecture, University of California, 1988), 24, 27–28.

9. Ibid., 24. For a summary of this period, see Melanie Simo, *100 Years*

of Landscape Architecture: Some Patterns of a Century (Washington, DC: ASLA Press, 1999), 89–128.

10. David C. Streatfield, *California Gardens: Creating a New Eden* (New York: Abbeville Press, 1994), 194.

11. Royston quoted in Laurie, *75 Years,* 28.

12. For more details on Vaughan, see Carrie Leah McDade, "Vaughan, Hollyngsworth Leland (1905–1974)," and "Vaughan, Adele Wharton," in *Shaping the American Landscape,* ed. Charles A. Birnbaum and Stephanie S. Foell (Charlottesville: University of Virginia Press, 2009), 360–62.

13. Royston, "A Landscape Architect," 217.

14. Interview by authors, July 13, 2006.

15. Interview by authors, January 18, 2003.

16. Ibid.

17. *Contemporary Landscape Architecture and Its Sources,* exhib. cat. (San Francisco Museum of Art, 1937), 15–19, 25.

18. Royston, "A Landscape Architect," 215–16. Arthur B. Hyde, son of the pioneering California horticulturalist H. A. Hyde, was a landscape architect and the proprietor of Hyde Nursery in Watsonville. Marie M. Harbeck, a 1932 graduate of Oregon State University's landscape architecture program, worked for Gardner A. Dailey before joining the Church firm. She married the landscape architect Arthur Berger in 1946, and the two operated a successful partnership throughout the South.

19. As a part-time employee in Church's office, Royston would have been familiar with Church's plans for the two gardens before they were constructed. Interview by authors, January 26, 2003. See also Marc Treib, "Maturity and Modernity," in *Thomas Church, Landscape Architect: Designing a Modern California Landscape,* ed. Marc Treib (San Francisco: William Stout, 2003), 95.

20. Dorothée Imbert, "Skewed Realities: The Garden and the Axonometric Drawing," in *Representing Landscape Architecture,* ed. Marc Treib (New York: Taylor & Francis, 2008), 135; Wendy Kaplan, *California Design, 1930–1965: Living in a Modern Way* (Cambridge: MIT Press, 2011), 167. Royston, "A Landscape Architect," 218.

21. Royston recalled realizing that these renowned modernist architects were also "talking about landscape architecture" through their design methodology. Royston, "A Landscape Architect," 217.

22. Interview by authors, March 14, 2002.

23. See Garrett Eckbo, Daniel U. Kiley, and James C. Rose, "Landscape Design in the Primeval Environment," *Architectural Record* 87 (February 1940): 74–79; "Landscape Design in the Rural Environment," *Architectural Record* 86 (August 1939): 68–74; and "Landscape Design in the Urban Environment," *Architectural Record* 85 (May 1939): 70–77.

24. Interview by authors, January 26, 2003. See also Serge Chermayeff, "Telesis: The Birth of a Group," *New Pencil Points,* July 1942, 45–48.

25. Royston, introduction to Garrett Eckbo, "Landscape Architecture: The Profession in California, 1935–1940, and Telesis," interview conducted in 1991 by Suzanne B. Riess, Regional Oral History Office, Bancroft Library, University of California, Berkeley, 1993, i.

26. Interview by authors, January 26, 2003.

27. See Dorothée Imbert, "Byways to Modernism: The Early Landscapes of Thomas Church," in Treib, *Thomas Church, Landscape Architect,* 19–71.

28. Royston quoted in John J. Wallace, "Robert Royston, Landscape Architect," master's thesis, University of California, Berkeley, 1992, 7.

29. Royston, "A Landscape Architect," 220.

30. Interview by authors, January 26, 2003.

31. Royston, "A Landscape Architect," 219.

32. Ibid., 223.

33. Royston in Eckbo, "Landscape Architecture," i.

34. Royston quoted in Wallace, "Robert Royston," 7.

35. Evelyn Beryl Dunwoody received a bachelor's degree in decorative arts from UC Berkeley, where she took graduate courses in landscape architecture. She was an industrial designer during the war and worked for Eckbo, Royston & Williams in the firm's early years. Obituary, *Independent Journal* [Marin County], March 8, 1980.

36. Interview by authors, January 26, 2003.

37. Royston in Eckbo, "Landscape Architecture," ii.

38. Robert Royston, "Point of View / Robert Royston," *Landscape Architecture* 76 (November–December 1986): 66.

39. Royston quoted in Wallace, "Robert Royston," 15.

40. See Kevin Starr, *Inventing the Dream: California through the Progressive Era* (New York: Oxford University Press, 1985).

41. See Mel Scott, *The San Francisco Bay Area: A Metropolis in Perspective,* 2nd ed. (Berkeley: University of California Press, 1985), 250–51, 271.

42. Robert N. Royston, "Is There a Bay Area Style?," *Architectural Record* 105 (May 1949): 96; Garrett Eckbo, *Landscape for Living,* reprint of 1950 ed. (Amherst: University of Massachusetts Press in association with Library of American Landscape History, 2009), 222–23. For a brief design analysis and plans of Ladera, see Marc Treib and Dorothée Imbert, *Garrett Eckbo: Modern Landscapes for Living* (Berkeley: University of California Press, 1997), 147–50.

43. Interview by authors, January 26, 2003.

44. For the Naify garden, see "Changing Levels Poses Few Problems," *Sunset,* February 1943, 24–25. The Wilson garden is illustrated in Joseph E. Howland, *The House Beautiful Book of Gardens and Outdoor Living* (New York: Doubleday, 1958), 56–57. The second Appert gar-

den was featured in several publications including John Hancock Callender, "Six West Coast Houses," *Architectural Record* 110 (November 1951): 124–25; Vance Bourjaily, "Serene and Livable Modern House," *San Francisco Chronicle,* March 12, 1950; and "Seven Outdoor Rooms Double the Living Space," *House & Garden,* August 1951, 30–31. Plans and descriptions of these gardens are located in the Robert N. Royston Collection, 1941–1990, Environmental Design Archives, College of Environmental Design, University of California, Berkeley (hereafter cited as RRC).

45. Interview by authors, March 14, 2002.

46. Ibid. and January 18, 2003.

47. Royston, "A Landscape Architect," 218. Popular as a textbook, *The Language of Vision* was reprinted thirteen times and translated into four languages.

48. Interview by authors, March 11, 2002.

49. According to Royston, several of the garden designs he created in the San Francisco division of the office are shown in Eckbo's *Landscape for Living,* including "Twin Gardens in Marin County, California, 1948" (142–43), his personal garden and the one he designed for Joseph Stein; "Garden in Woodside Hills, California, 1947" (154–55), commissioned by the Naify family; "Country Home in Marin County, California, 1946" (158–59); and "Ranch Home in Central Valley of California, 1945" (158–59). Interview by authors, March 14, 2002.

50. For representative examples of the work of Bay Area landscape architects from the 1940s and 1950s, see the exhibition catalogs *Landscape Design 1948* (San Francisco Museum of Art and Association of Landscape Architects, 1948) and *Landscape Architecture 1958,* ed. R. Burton Litton Jr. (San Francisco Museum of Art, 1958). For a brief account of the period, see Laurie, *75 Years of Landscape Architecture,* chaps. 4 and 5.

51. American Public Health Association, Committee on the Hygiene of Housing, *Planning the Neighborhood: Standards for Healthful Housing* (Chicago: Public Administration Service, 1948). The book's emphasis on neighborhood units influenced the planning commissions of Palo Alto and Santa Clara, where Royston designed some of his most important parks.

52. See Arthur B. Gallion and Simon Eisner, *The Urban Pattern: City Planning and Design* (New York: D. Van Nostrand, 1963), 250–54. Gallion and Eisner refer to N. L. Engelhardt Jr., "The School Neighborhood Nucleus," *Architectural Forum* 79 (October 1943): 88–91, and Clarence Arthur Perry, *The Neighborhood Unit,* monograph 1 of *Neighborhood and Community Planning,* vol. 7 of *Regional Survey of New York and Its Environs* (New York, 1929).

53. See John Keats, *The Crack in the Picture Window* (Boston: Houghton

Mifflin, 1957), and Richard E. Gordon et al., *The Split-Level Trap* (New York: B. Geis Associates, 1961).

54. Deborah Bishop, "Avant Gardens," *Dwell,* September 2007, 128.

55. Interview by authors, March 14, 2002. Original plans of the Rod & Gun Club are located in RRC.

56. The Chinn garden is featured in "Color and Texture," *Sunset,* August 1955, 44.

57. He taught at North Carolina State in 1952, 1954, and 1957. Interview by authors, March 14, 2002.

58. Plans and descriptions of these projects are located in RRC.

59. Interview by authors, January 26, 2003. See also Robert N. Royston, "A Brief History," *Landscape Australia* 8 (Fall 1986): 34–36, 38.

60. Royston quoted in Wallace, "Robert Royston," 18. He gave a similar definition during an interview by the authors, January 18, 2003.

61. California Committee on Planning for Recreation, Park Areas and Facilities, *Guide for Planning Recreation Parks in California: A Basis for Determining Local Recreation Space* (Sacramento: Printing Division, Documents Section, 1956). The committee included two landscape architects, the Bay Area practitioner Theodore Osmundson Jr. and William Penn Mott Jr., superintendent of parks, Oakland.

62. Interviews by authors, July 10, 2002; January 26, 2003; and August 8, 2003 (quote).

63. Interview by authors, March 4, 2002. For an excellent analysis of playground design in the post–World War II era, see Susan G. Solomon, *American Playgrounds: Revitalizing Community Space* (Lebanon, NH: University Press of New England, 2005), chaps. 1–2.

64. Solomon, *American Playgrounds,* 35.

65. "Palo Alto's Mitchell Park, A West Coast Design Leader," *American City* 72 (November 1957): 29; see Rainey and Miller, *Modern Public Gardens,* 97.

66. Carlisle would become an associate of the firm in 1963 and a principal ten years later. Alley became a principal in 1979.

67. Interview by authors, July 27, 2003.

68. Ibid.

69. Paul Adamson and Marty Arbunich, *Eichler: Modernism Rebuilds the American Dream* (Layton, UT: Gibbs Smith, 2002).

70. Plans of these projects are located in RRC.

71. Interview by authors, January 26, 2003.

72. Plans are located in RRC.

73. In 2016, the university announced plans to restore the amphitheater, and students agreed to the use of over $6 million in student fees to support the project. See Scott Hernandez-Jason, "Campus to Kick-off Quarry Amphitheater Restoration," October 31, 2016, UCSC Newscenter, http://news.ucsc.edu/2016/10/quarry-restoration.html.

74. Royston, Hanamoto, Beck & Abey, undated promotional brochure, JC Miller private collection.

75. Lawrence Livermore National Laboratory timeline, "The 1960s," www.llnl.gov/archives/1960s#22.

76. Harold Watkin, "A Landscape Contractor Evokes Student Days in the 1930s, and Discusses His Own Profession, in *Thomas Church, Landscape Architect,* 2 vols., interviews conducted by Suzanne B. Riess, Regional Oral History Office, Bancroft Library, University of California, Berkeley (Watkin interview, January 29, 1975), 1:65.

77. Royston, Hanamoto, Beck & Alley, "Preliminary Information Base Analysis, South Portion of Golden Gate National Recreation Area, San Francisco, CA," prepared for GGNRA, US Department of the Interior, 1975; RHBA, "Quantification of Potential Visitor Use under Park Alternatives," GGNRA, Fort Mason, CA, 1976; RHBA and GFDS Engineers, "Safety Hazard Study, Alcatraz Island," GGNRA, National Park Service, 1979.

78. See Academy of Art University, School of Landscape Architecture, "Spotlight: RHAA Celebrates the National Park Service Centennial," blog, March 28, 2016, www.landscapearchitecturedaily.com.

79. Beck became widely known for his concept design of Whistler Village, British Columbia, a ski resort developed in the late 1970s that was the site of the 2010 Winter Olympics. He went on to establish his own firm, Eldon Beck Associates, and to gain prominence as the designer of environmentally sensitive and engaging "resort landscapes" for ski areas, including Keystone and Copper Mountain, Colorado; Mammoth and Squaw Valley, California; and Stratton Mountain, Vermont.

80. "Royston, Hanamoto, Alley & Abey," undated promotional booklet, JC Miller private collection. These were the days when a bachelor's degree was sufficient to establish professional credibility, whether one taught or practiced. Only four individuals in RHAA had degrees above the bachelor's level, and of the seven principals only one architect, Louis Alley, had earned a master's degree.

81. Plans of these projects and the firm's other international commissions are in RRC.

82. Royston, drafts of two *Landscape Australia* articles, JC Miller private collection. These comments were not published in the final versions: "A Brief History" and "Robert Royston's Thoughts on Landscape Architecture," *Landscape Australia* 8 (Fall 1986): 34–36 and (Winter 1986): 152–54.

83. Interview by authors, January 26, 2003.

84. Ibid.

85. Royston, "A Brief History," 38.

86. Royston, "Robert Royston's Thoughts," 154.

87. Royston to Ervin H. Zube, Professor of Landscape Architecture, University of Arizona, [n.d.], 1990, RRC.
88. Interview by authors, July 27, 2003.
89. Ibid.
90. JC Miller worked with Royston on this project—gardens for two homes owned by Brent Harris and Lisa Meulbroek Harris—in 2008. "A Suite of Gardens—Palm Springs, CA," JC Miller private collection.
91. Royston, "A Brief History," 38.
92. Reuben M. Rainey and JC Miller, "Royston, Robert (1918–2008), Landscape Architect, Educator," in Birnbaum and Foell, *Shaping the American Landscape,* 300.

LADERA

1. Interview by authors, March 14, 2002.
2. James Murray Luck, *Reminiscences,* James Murray Luck Memorial Fund, Annual Reviews, Palo Alto, CA, 1999, available at www.annualreviews.org.
3. Ibid., 76.
4. Peninsula Housing Authority, *Your Home in Ladera* (1947). See Steven White, *Building the Garden: The Architecture of Joseph Allen Stein in India and California* (New York: Oxford University Press, 1993), 94–95.
5. Garrett Eckbo, *Landscape for Living,* reprint of 1950 ed. (Amherst: University of Massachusetts Press in association with Library of American Landscape History, 2009), 223. See also Mark Treib and Dorothée Imbert, *Garrett Eckbo: Modern Landscapes for Living* (Berkeley: University of California Press, 1997), 147–50.
6. John Funk, "An Architect Looks at Co-op Housing," *CO-OP Magazine,* January 1947, 14–17.
7. White, *Building in the Garden,* 81–83, 92–97; interviews by authors, March 14, 2002, and January 26, 2003.
8. Interview by authors, January 26, 2003.
9. Treib and Imbert, *Garrett Eckbo,* 133–41.
10. See plans of selected playgrounds in Eckbo, *Landscape for Living,* 222–23.
11. Treib and Imbert, *Garret Eckbo,* 150.

ROYSTON AND STEIN GARDENS

1. The homes received immediate attention, appearing in both *Architectural Forum* and *Arts & Architecture* magazines by mid-1949. Concurrently, Royston's garden designs drew critical praise and were published frequently, first in the *San Francisco Chronicle* and *Marin Independent Journal* and later in *Sunset* magazine. The gardens also appeared through-

out the 1950s in homeowner-oriented books by Lane Publishing, the parent company of *Sunset.*

2. See "Twin Houses: Berkeley, California," *Progressive Architecture,* March 1951, 83–87, available at www.usmodernist.org.

3. Stephen White, *Building in the Garden: The Architecture of Joseph Allen Stein in India and California* (New York: Oxford University Press, 1993), 50.

4. "Low Cost House," *Architectural Forum* 73 (October 1940): 264–65, available at www.usmodernist.org.

5. White, *Building in the Garden,* 62.

6. See "Design in Plant & Structure," *Sunset,* June 1950, 92; "The Vertical Garden," *Sunset,* July 1950, 78, 110; "Plantings Can Extend the Walls of the Western Home," *Sunset,* February 1951, 83; and "Surprise Companions," *Sunset,* February 1952, 106.

7. With the end of shipbuilding in the Bay Area, Haydite was inexpensive and readily available, while more traditional materials were scarce. For a description of the material and its uses, see www.digagg.com/about_us/.

8. Interview by authors, July 16, 2006.

9. One of Royston's study drawings for the garden appears in Garret Eckbo's *Landscape for Living,* published in 1950. The screen in Royston's imagination was considerably longer and incorporated more of Swift's tiles than the structure as built.

STANDARD OIL ROD & GUN CLUB PARK

1. Interview by authors, January 26, 2002.

2. Ibid.

3. Interview by authors, July 9, 2002.

4. *Pacific Architect & Builder* featured the large slide on its cover, and an article, "For Employees: Relaxation in the Sun or Shade," praised the park for its innovative design. See *Pacific Architect & Builder,* December 1957, 18–20.

5. See R. Burton Litton Jr., "Designing Parks for Children," *Parks & Recreation* 42 (June 1959): 272–74; "Playgrounds Have Discovered Design," *Architectural Record* 115 (January 1954): 155–56. The project was also included in an exhibition at the San Francisco Museum of Art: *Landscape Architecture 1958,* ed. R. Burton Litton Jr. (San Francisco Museum of Art, 1958).

6. Robert N. Royston, "Standard's Employees Do It Themselves," *Landscape Architecture* 55 (October 1964): 55–56.

7. Interview by authors, January 26, 2002.

SECOND APPERT GARDEN

1. In 1959, when Lenkurt Electric merged with General Telephone and Kurt semiretired, the Apperts commissioned Royston to create a landscape for their third house, in Woodside, designed by the architect Henry Hill. See Kurt E. Appert, "Electrical Engineering and the Lenkurt Electric Company," interview conducted by Art Norborg, September 25, 1974, Oral History Center, Bancroft Library, University of California, Berkeley, 1982.
2. Interview by authors, November 15, 2004.
3. Ibid.
4. See "Seven Outdoor Rooms Double the Living Space," *House & Garden,* August 1951, 30–31; Vance Bourjaily, "Serene and Livable Modern House," *San Francisco Chronicle,* March 12, 1950; John Hancock Callender, "Six West Coast Houses," *Architectural Record* 110 (November 1951): 124–25.

CHINN GARDEN

1. Interview by authors, July 16, 2006.
2. Ibid.
3. Steven C. Pepper, "Introduction to Garden Design," *Landscape Design 1948* (San Francisco Museum of Art and Association of Landscape Architects, 1948), 5. Pepper notes, "The creation of a garden becomes something halfway between the making of a painting and the making of a house. It is as if the landscape architect were composing an abstract painting for people to live within. And because people are to live inside it . . . the functions it is to serve as a place to dig, to dine, to play games in, or read in, or nap in become also elements of its composition."
4. See "Color and Texture," *Sunset,* August 1955, 44; Richard Neutra, "The Patio House: An Ancient Concept That Can Solve a Modern Problem," *House & Home,* August 1956, 127, 196. A photo of the garden appeared in *House & Garden,* February 1956, 101.

KRUSI PARK PLAYGROUND

1. American Public Health Association, Committee on the Hygiene of Housing, *Planning the Neighborhood: Standards for Healthful Housing* (Chicago: Public Administration Service, 1948), v–vii, 1–3.
2. "Design Decade: Playground Equipment," *Architectural Record* 73 (October 1940): 245.
3. William Penn Mott Jr., "Children's Fairyland," *Parks & Recreation* 34 (March 1951): 5–7; and William Penn Mott, Jr., "Magic Key to Your Park's Story," *Parks & Recreation* 42 (May 1959): 220–22. Frank Caplan, president of Play-Sculptures, Inc., which manufactured abstract sculp-

tural play apparatuses, also criticized the Fairyland approach for limiting a child's imagination. Caplan, "The Playgrounds of Tomorrow," *Parks & Recreation* 43 (January 1960): 18–20.

4. Interview by authors, January 26, 2003.
5. Ibid.
6. *Landscape Architecture 1958,* ed. R. Burton Litton Jr., exhib. cat. (San Francisco Museum of Art, 1958).

MITCHELL PARK

1. For information about the cost of the park, see Elizabeth L. Hogan, ed., *Parks of Palo Alto* (Palo Alto Historical Association, 1966), 31–33.
2. American Public Health Association, Committee on the Hygiene of Housing, *Planning the Neighborhood: Standards for Healthful Housing* (Chicago: Public Administration Service, 1948).
3. *Guide for Planning Recreation Parks in California: A Basis for Determining Local Recreation Space* (Sacramento: Printing Division, Documents Section, 1956).
4. A photograph of the bears appeared in *Landscape Architecture 1958,* ed. R. Burton Litton Jr. (San Francisco Museum of Art, 1958), 32.
5. Hogan, *Parks of Palo Alto,* 48.
6. Interview by authors, March 14, 2002.
7. Interview by authors, January 26, 2003.
8. Only one copy of the film was made. It circulated among local chapters of the American Society of Landscape Architects. The digitized version is available in RRC.

ST. MARY'S SQUARE

1. Plans and photographs of St. Mary's Square are in RRC.
2. Henry J. Degenklob, "St. Mary's Square Underground Garage," *Architect and Engineer* 197 (May 1954): 11–17, 33–34; see also "To Relieve the Parking Headache," *P.G. and E. Progress* 30 (September 1953): 1–2.
3. Interview by authors, March 14, 2002.
4. Degenklob, "St. Mary's Square," 11–17.
5. Interview by authors, March 14, 2002.
6. Ibid.

CENTRAL PARK

1. In a letter to Elizabeth Muffeny of the AIA, Carmichael recommended Royston for an Allied Professionals Award, describing him as "one of the finest men that I have had the opportunity to work with and to know. . . . I know him, not only as a very capable professional

landscape architect, planner and environmentalist, but also, as a very wonderful, kind human being and very close personal friend" (July 24, 1990, RRC).

2. Interview by authors, March 9, 2003.
3. "Report on a General Plan for the City of Santa Clara, California, 1959," 18–22, copy in Bancroft Library, University of California, Berkeley.
4. Interview by authors and tour of Central Park, July 9, 2002.
5. "All-City Picnic and Dedication of Central Park, Saturday, August 10, 1974," City of Santa Clara Parks and Recreation Department, 1974, RHAA.
6. In 1970, Central Park received an Environmental Planning Award from the California Park and Recreation Society and, in 1974, an honor award from the AIA. Earl Carmichael also published articles on Central Park as part of the overall Santa Clara park system. See Carmichael, "Make Your Parks People-Pleasers," *American City,* April 1964, 98–100, and "Park Plans Can Simplify Maintenance," *American City,* October 1966, 104–6.

STANFORD LINEAR ACCELERATOR CAMPUS

1. SLAC press release, March 16, 1962, RHMB office file, RCC.
2. R. B. Neal, ed., *The Stanford Two-Mile Accelerator* (New York: W. A. Benjamin, 1968), 28–29.
3. In a conversation with the authors recorded on July 13, 2006, Royston explains how he came to know Edward Ginzton and through that connection eventually became associated with the SLAC project.
4. Stanford Linear Accelerator Center Landscape Program, approved by Stanford Board of Trustees, July 1962. A photocopy of this report, along with a site plan graphic, was received by the RHMB office in September 1962, RCC.
5. See RHMB contract documents, RCC.
6. Robert Royston/RHMB to MHL Sanders, Director of Planning, Stanford University, memo including proposed plant list, November 1, 1962, RHMB office file, RCC.
7. Minutes from joint meeting of Engineering Committee and Architectural Advisory Council, September 20, 1962, EDA.

SANTA CLARA CIVIC CENTER PARK

1. Plans and photographs of the park are held in RRC.
2. Interview by authors, July 10, 2002.
3. "Santa Clara Civic Center Park" files, RRC.
4. Interview by authors, July 10, 2002.

5. The redwood in Palo Alto's Mitchell Park, Royston's only previous use of plant symbolism, was a "tall tree" emblematic of the city's Spanish name.
6. Interview by authors, July 10, 2002.

ESTATES RESERVOIR
1. J. W. Noble, *Its Name Was M.U.D.: A Story of Water* (Oakland: [East Bay Municipal Utility District], 1999), 38.
2. EBMUD, "General Plan of Reservoir and Dam 175-R," 1938.
3. RHMB project description memos, March 1964, on file in RRC.
4. Ibid.
5. Interview by authors, July 18, 2006.
6. EBMUD, "Estates Reservoir Replacement Draft Environmental Impact Report," 2009. See www.ebmud.com/about-us/construction-my-neighborhood/estates-reservoir-replacement/.

SUNRIVER
1. Interview by authors, March 14, 2002.
2. Sunriver Properties, *Sunriver* promotional booklet, 1970, RRC.
3. Ibid.; interview by authors, March 14, 2002.
4. Sunriver Properties, *Sunriver.*
5. Interview by authors, July 10, 2002.
6. Ibid.
7. For commentary on Sunriver's natural environment and health benefits, see Barbara Plumb, "Pollution Free Paradise," *American Home*, January 1971, 33–39, and Dolly Connelly, "The Healthiest New Town in America," clipping, RRC.

SAN JOAQUIN DELTA COLLEGE
1. The RRC contains extensive records of the firm's work on three major campus projects: California State University, Stanislaus College, 1963–1980s; University of California, San Francisco, 1958–1973; and the University of Utah, 1957–1973. More limited records are held of the campuses for Bethel College, Newton, KS, 1961; St. Benedict's College, Atchison, KS, 1961; Mills College, San Francisco, 1962; Park College, Parkville, MO, 1962; City College of San Francisco, 1965; University of California, Santa Cruz, Merrill College, 1965–67; Weber College, Ogden, UT, 1966; Foothill College, Los Altos, 1968; Illinois Valley Community College, Oglesby, IL,1968; Lassen Community College, Susanville, CA, 1968; Parkland College, Champaign, IL, 1968; Westminster College, Salt Lake City, UT, 1968.

2. See California Community Colleges Chancellor's Office website, www.ccccco.edu/.

3. RHAA promotional booklet, n.d., JC Miller private collection.

4. Robert Royston was on sabbatical during the project's design phase but visited the office to comment on the design. He approved its final version in a formal meeting with the partners at RHBA. Harold Kobayashi, interview by authors, August 31, 2016.

5. San Joaquin Delta College Catalog, 2017–2018, available at https://archive.deltacollege.edu/dept/ar/catalog/catalog_main.html.

6. Beck was well versed in these ideas through his association with the Department of Landscape Architecture at UC Berkeley, as a part-time lecturer from 1965 to 1977 and an adjunct professor from 1978 to 1985. Michael Laurie with David Streatfield, *75 Years of Landscape Architecture at Berkeley: An Informal History / Part II: Recent Years* (Department of Landscape Architecture, University of California, Berkeley, 1992), 67–68.

7. Eldon Beck, interview by JC Miller, September 24, 2016.

8. Ibid.

9. Despite remarkable displays of wildflowers during the first three springs, the planting on the berms was changed to a mixture of native and non-native groundcover shrubs owing to a combination of aesthetic concerns (the berms were thought to be too wild-looking by late summer) and the practicalities of institutional maintenance.

10. Richard R. Williams, *The Physical Development of Sangamon State University, 1969–1995* (Springfield, IL: Sangamon State University, 1995), 9–10.

RIVERSIDE NATIONAL CEMETERY

1. Harold N. Kobayashi, interview by authors, August 31, 2016.

2. Louis G. Alley, "From Air Force Wasteland a New V.A. Cemetery," *Landscape Architecture* 68 (March 1978): 129, 131; Louis Alley, interview by authors, September 28, 2016.

3. Kobayashi interview.

4. Royston, Hanamoto, Alley & Abey, promotional booklet, n.d., JC Miller private collection.

5. For a history of memorial park cemeteries, see David Charles Sloane, *The Last Great Necessity: Cemeteries in American History* (Baltimore: Johns Hopkins University Press, 1991), chaps. 7 and 9.

6. RHAA promotional booklet.

7. Louis Alley, interview by authors, September 29, 2016.

8. See U.S. Department of Veterans Affairs, National Cemetery Administration, "Riverside National Cemetery," www.cem.va.gov/CEM/cems/nchp/riverside.asp.

HARRIS GARDEN

1. Authors' conversation with Royston, December 2006. During the conceptual and design development phases of the project, about January 2007 through the summer of 2008, when declining health prohibited his working, Royston and Miller met regularly to review progress. During their meetings, Royston would make sketches and explain his ideas and intentions for the garden. Miller would then return to the RHAA office, where he and his team would update the plan and develop details. A weeklong visit to Palm Springs that included a rented Lincoln Town Car was a highlight of their work together on the project. Many of Royston and Miller's conversations were recorded, and unless indicated otherwise, quotations are drawn from those recordings.

2. During an early design meeting in 2007, Royston went to his library and retrieved his copy of Will Grohmann's *Wassily Kandinsky, Life and Work*. Opening it to a full-page illustration of *Several Circles* that he had previously marked, he declared, "This is our garden."

INDEX

and Urban Development Department

Howard, Ebenezer, influence on Royston, 33

Hubbard, Henry, *Introduction to the Study of Landscape Design,* 13

Hudson, Tom and Allen, Royston's design for residences (Berkeley), 72

Hunter's Point (San Francisco Redevelopment Agency), Royston's plan for, 42

Hyde, Arthur B. (landscape architect), 246n18; Royston's student work with, 14

Hyde, Henry Alton (horticulturalist), 246n18

Igaz, Rudolf (architect), and St. Mary's Square project, 142

Ingels, James (Royston firm member), 242–43

International Recreation Congress (1958), and Mitchell Park, 37

International School, and modern design, 15, 246n21

Introduction to the Study of Landscape Design, An (Hubbard and Kimball), 13

isometric plans and drawings: Krusi Park Playground, *118;* Mitchell Park, "tiny tot playground," *130;* Naify garden, *6;* second Appert garden, *100;* Standard Oil Rod & Gun Club Park, *90*

Japan, flood control projects in, 50

JJR (landscape architecture firm), 38

Johnson, Bill (landscape architect), 38

Johnson, Carl (landscape architect), 38

Jones & Emmons (architects), and Eichler Homes projects, 40

Jordan Quad, Stanford University, Royston's design for, 41

Jurong Bird Park (Singapore), RHAA design for, 50

Kandinsky, Wassily: Royston's interest in, 16; *Several Circles,* and Harris garden design, 56, 233, 258n2

Kaohsiung Metropolitan Park (Taiwan), RHAA design for, 50

Kassabaum, George (architect), 38

Kent, T. J., Jr. (city planner), and Telesis, 17

Kepes, Gyorgy, *The Language of Vision,* 26, 248n47

Keystone (ski resort; Keystone, CO), Beck's design for, 250n79

Kiley, Dan, articles in *Pencil Points* and *Architectural Record,* 12, 17

Kimball, Theodora, *Introduction to the Study of Landscape Design,* 13

King, Manuela (Royston firm member), 242–43

Klystron Gallery. *See under* Stanford Linear Accelerator Campus

Kobayashi, Harold (Royston firm member), 242; and Central Park (Santa Clara), 152; role in RHBA, 44; and San Joaquin Delta College design, 202

Krusi Park Playground: (Alameda, CA): age zones, 119; climbing structures, *120, 122;* fencing, 117–18; influence of, 125; isometric sketch, *118;* and Mitchell Park design, 37;

older children's area, 121–25; pedal car freeway and gas station, 118, 122–23, *122, 123, 124;* play equipment, 35, 37, 117, 119–23; and playgrounds and play equipment as art, 117, 122; and Royston's use of improvisation, 121; site plan, 117–18; and theories on play, 118–19; "Tiny Tot Area," *118,* 119–21, *121*

Kuala Lumpur, Malaysia, National Heroes Cemetery, RHBA design for, 50, 225

Kump Associates. *See* Ernest J. Kump Associates

Ladera cooperative housing (San Mateo County, CA), 23; and "California Contemporary" style, 68; Eckbo and, 23, 61, 65; and economic and racial diversity, 62, 69; failure of, 23, 69; and Federal Housing Authority, 69; Ginzton and, 164; housing types and landscape designs, *65, 66–68, 66, 67;* and landscape matrix concept, 61, 68; linear park and recreation facilities, 68; and Lucas Valley design, 41; model, *63;* pedestrian paths, 68; and *Planning the Neighborhood,* 33; planting plans, 68; playgrounds, *64,* 68–69; Royston's involvement in, 61, 69; setting and topography, 62–65; site plan, *60,* 68; size, 23, 69

landscape architecture, development of profession, 250n80

landscape architecture firms: and New Deal public works programs, 11; studio and corporate models of, 38; postwar changes, 4–5, 11–12; transition to larger-scale projects in 1950s, 37–38

Landscape Architecture 1958 (San Francisco Museum of Modern Art) exhibition catalog, and Krusi Park Playground, 125; and Standard Oil Rod & Gun Club Park, 252n5

landscape as visual experience: in Royston's park designs, 6; and Santa Clara Civic Center Park, 185; and Estates Reservoir project, 182, 185

Landscape Australia, Royston's articles for, 52–53

Landscape for Living (Eckbo), 28; Royston's garden designs in, *80*, 248n49

landscape matrix, Royston's concept of, 23, 33–34; and campus designs, 34, 46, 201–2; and city planning, 34; and environmental concerns, 213; and Estates Reservoir and other reservoir covers, 181; and Harris garden, 230–31; and Ladera, 61, 68; and North Bonneville, WA, design, 48; and park design, 33, 53; regional environment as largest element of, 49, 59; and San Joaquin Delta College design, 202, 213; and Sunriver, 189, 196, 198–99; and Vail, CO, project, 48

Language of Vision, The (Kepes), 26, 248n47

Lawrence Radiation Laboratory (Livermore, CA; now

Lawrence Livermore National Laboratory), RHBA development plan for, 33, 47

Le Corbusier, influence on Royston, 15, 246n21

Ledermann, Alfred (child welfare advocate), and playground design, 34

Leland King & Associates (architectural firm), and Riverside National Cemetery project, 216, 221

Lenkurt Electric Company, 101, 253n1

Litton, R. B., Jr., 28

Loran, Erle (artist; UC Berkeley professor), influence on Royston, 13–14

Los Alamos National Laboratory, master plan for, 50

Lozier, Nathan (Royston firm member), 242–43

Lucas Valley planned community (Marin County, CA), master plan for, 41, *41*

Luck, James Murray, and Ladera, 61–62

Lundburg, Barbara (Royston firm member), 242–43

Machotka, Danielle and Julia Anne (daughters of Hannelore Gothe Royston), 52

Malaysia, projects in, 4, 8, 50, 225

Mammoth Mountain (ski resort; Mammoth Lakes, CA), Beck's design for, 250n79

March Air Force Base (Riverside County, CA), and Riverside National Cemetery, 215–16

Massachusetts Agricultural College (now University of Massachusetts Amherst), 11

Matsumoto, George (architect),

and Central Park (Santa Clara) community center, 160

Mayes, David R. (Royston firm member), 241; and Central Park (Santa Clara), 152; joins Eckbo, Royston & Williams, 26; joins Royston, Hanamoto & Mayes, 6–7, 37; leaves firm, 43; and Santa Clara Civic Center Park, 175

McCallum, Donald V. (developer), and Sunriver, 189–90

"memorial park" cemetery designs, 216–17

Merrill College (UC Santa Cruz), RHBA design for, 46

Metropolitan Insurance Company, Park Merced housing project (San Francisco), Royston's involvement in, 19

Mexico, projects in, 4

Mies van der Rohe, Ludwig, influence on Royston, 15, 246n21

Miller, JC (Royston firm member), 242; and Harris garden, 227, 231, 251n90, 258n1

Mitchell Park (Palo Alto, CA): apartment house climbing structure, 133, *134;* bear sculptures by Virginia Green, 55, 133, *137;* berms, 37, 130, *132,* 133; garden tables 56–57; "gopher holes," 133, *135;* innovations of, 36–37; Magical Bridge playground (RHAA, 2016), 139; multi-use slab, *37,* 128, *128, 132;* pedal car freeway, 133, *136;* pergolas, 138; picnic area, 130, *131, 132, 137;* planting plan, 56, 136–38; play equipment, 55, 128; playground, 55; as precedent-setting public space,

Royston firm, 241–43; Eckbo, Royston & Williams, formation, of, 5; growth of, 8–9; influence of, 8; international offices, 50–52; Mill Valley office, 242; as modernist firm, 5; range and scope of work, 4, 42, 50, 256n1; Royston, Hanamoto, Alley & Abey, formation of, 50; Royston, Hanamoto, Beck & Abey, formation of, 43–44; Royston, Hanamoto & Mayes, formation of, 6–7, 37; Royston, Hanamoto, Mayes & Beck, formation of, 42; Royston's involvement in firm's projects, 52; San Francisco and Los Angeles offices, 23; shift to corporate model, 3, 38; structure of, 243. *See also under individual firm names*

Salt Lake City, projects in, 4
San Francisco Chronicle, and second Appert garden, 109
San Francisco Museum of Art, *Design in the Patio* exhibition: ERW's work at, 78; Royston garden screen in, *80*
San Francisco Museum of Art, *Houses for War and Post-War* exhibit, Stein's work in, 74
San Francisco Museum of Modern Art, *Landscape Architecture 1958* exhibition catalog: and Krusi Park Playground, 125; and Standard Oil Rod & Gun Club Park, 252n5
San Francisco Parking Authority, and St. Mary's Square project, 141
San Francisco Recreation and

Parks Commission, and St. Mary's Square project, 141
San Francisco Redevelopment Agency, projects for, 42
Sangamon State University (Springfield, IL; now University of Illinois Springfield), campus plan by RHBA and Murphy, Downey, Wofford & Richman, 211
San Joaquin Delta College (Stockton, CA), *205;* as "acropolis plan," 209; berms, 47, 206–8, *207, 208,* 257n9; campus core diagram, *203;* campus core path, *210;* central courtyard, 208; central quad pond, *209;* courtyards and steps, 202, *204, 212;* design team, 46, 202; and diversity, 202; division into "instructional centers," 202; drainage and flood control, 205, 208; and environmental concerns, 47, 208; expansion (1973), 209; fountain terrace, *211;* Holt courtyard, *212;* influence of, 213; and landscape matrix concept, 202, 213; parking lots and ring road, 46–47, *205,* 206, *207,* 208; pedestrian central campus, 46–47, 205–7; pedestrian pathways, 47, 206, *206,* 208; plantings, 47, 208; pond, 208; Royston's involvement in, 257n4; site history, 204–5; site plan by Kump Associates, modifications by RHBA, 46, *200,* 202–4, 208; use of native plants, *205,* 208, 257n9; waterfall, *209*

Santa Barbara, CA, Royston's model of, 10
Santa Clara Civic Center Park (Santa Clara, CA), *175;* amphitheater, 175; berms, 174–75; Carmichael and, 173; and experience of space, 39; footbridge, *177;* and landscape as visual experience, 39, 185; olive trees, 178; paths, 39, 173–74; planters and flowerbeds, 174; planting plan, 39, 175–77, *176;* pools and fountain, 174; preservation of, 179; site challenges, 173; site plan, *172,* 173–74; St. Clare statute (Van Kleeck), 39, 174, 178–79, *178;* use of color, 174, 177; as water parterre, 173
Santiago, Chile, Parque del Recuerdo cemetery, RHAA design for, 50, *51,* 225
Sasaki, Hideo (landscape architect), 38
Sasaki, Walker & Associates, and Foothill College (Los Altos Hills, CA), 207
School of Dentistry, UC San Francisco, RHBA site plan for, 211
School of Public Health, UC Berkeley, Royston's design for, 32
Schultze, Leonard (architect), 19
Scott, Geraldine Knight (landscape architect), and Telesis, 17; and UC Berkeley Department of Landscape Architecture, 28
second Appert garden (Atherton, CA): Bourjaily on, 109; collaboration with Stein, 102–3; coast live oaks, 103, *103;* entry patio and loggia,

second Appert garden (*continued*) *104,* 105; hardscape, 105–6; influence of, 25, 108–9; isometric drawing, *100;* model, *108;* planting plan, 105, 108; site challenges, 103; site plan for house and gardens, *102,* 103–5; Stein design for house, 101–3, *103,* 105; swimming pool, 105–6, *106;* terrace, 25, 103, 105–8, *107;* use of color, 105, 107–9; use of native plants, 103; use of texture, 109

Several Circles (Kandinsky), and Harris garden design, 56, 233, 258n2

Shepherd, Harry (UC Berkeley Landscape Design program), 13

Silicon Valley, RHMB projects in, 42–43

Singapore, projects in, 4, 50

space, concept and experience of: elements of spatial experience, 54–55; in Harris garden, 230–31, 235; and International School architectural designs, 15; and Kepes's *Language of Vision,* 26; in Krusi Park Playground, 118; and landscape matrix, 33; in Mitchell Park, 138; and plantings, 7, 39, 69, 97, 136; as primary medium, 5, 7–8; psychological effects of, 10, 39, 40; in Santa Clara Civic Center Park, 39, 177; in second Appert garden, 109; in Standard Oil Rod & Gun Club Park, 89, 97; and study models, 27; and use of berms, 37

Space (student publication, UC

Berkeley Landscape Design program), 27

Squaw Valley (ski resort; Olympic Valley, CA), Beck's design for, 250n79

Standard Oil refinery (Port Richmond, CA), 89

Standard Oil Rod & Gun Club Park (Point Richmond, CA): collaboration with company executives and workers, 89, 99; docks, 89; hardscape, 95; influence of, 97–99, 252n5; isometric plan, *90;* and maintenance concerns, 95; and Mitchell Park design, 36; parking lot, 89; pedestrian paths, 90–91; pergolas, 30, 93, *94;* planting plan, 91–93, 97; playgrounds and play equipment, 95, *96, 97, 98,* 99; pedestrian paths, 90–91; picnic area, 95; recreational zones, 90–92; Royston article on, 97–99; and Royston's view of park design, 29–30, 89, 99; screens used as windbreaks and suntraps, 30, 56, 93, *93,* 237; site and concept plan, 89–91, *91;* swimming and wading pools, *88,* 91–93, *92, 94;* use of garden elements, 30, 95, 99; use of native plants, 90, 97; use of vegetation to define space, 97

Stanford Linear Accelerator Campus (SLAC; Menlo Park, CA), *162, 170;* and accelerator development, 163–64; Klystron Gallery, challenges of, 163, 167–68, 170; landscape master plan, *166;* lantern lights, *169;* master

plan by Stanford staff, 164–67; master plan revision by RHMB, 38, 167–69; nursery program, 171; path system, 167; plantings, *165,* 167–68; use of fieldstone, 169–70; use of native plants, 168

Stanford University, Church's designs for, 168–70

Stanford University, Jordan Quad, Royston's design for, 41

Stanford University, particle physics and accelerator science programs, 163–64. *See also* Stanford Linear Accelerator Campus

Stanislaus College (Turlock, CA; now California State University, Stanislaus), RHBA design for, 45–46

Steele, Fletcher (landscape architect), design of Naumkeag (Mabel Choate estate), 12

Stegner, Wallace (novelist), on Ladera, 62

Stein, Joseph Allen (architect): early residential designs, 73–74; design for second Appert house (Atherton, CA), 25, 101–5, *103;* in *Houses for War and Post-War* exhibit (San Francisco Museum of Art), 74; Ladera housing designs, 62, *65, 66, 67,* 66–68; named head of Department of Architecture at Bengal Engineering College, Calcutta, 76; in Neutra's office, 73–74; and Telesis, 17, 71; work shown in *Architectural Forum,* 74; and Wurster, 73. *See also* second Appert garden; Royston and Stein gardens

St. Louis, projects in, 4

St. Mary's Cathedral (San Francisco), and St. Mary's Square project, 142–43, *146*

St. Mary's Square (San Francisco), *143, 145, 146;* and Chinatown location, 30, 141, 145–46, 149; collaboration with Rudolf Igaz (architect) and John J. Gould (engineer), 141–42, 145; curvilinear elements, 145, 148; as early rooftop square, 141; garage structure, 31, 141–42; hardscape, 146–48, *147;* lawn areas, 145, *147;* park plaza sketch, *142;* Pine Street entry, *148;* planters, 145, 148–49; planting plan, 149; restoration and additions in 1990s, 149; seating, *30, 146,* 148; site plan, 143–45; and St. Mary's Cathedral, 142–43, *146;* Sun Yat-sen statue, *30,* 143, *144,* 146–48; use of color and texture, 149; walkways, 148

Stockton State Hospital (Stockton, CA), 205

Stratton (ski resort; Stratton Mountain, VT), Beck's design for, 250n79

Sunriver (Deschutes County, OR): and Camp Abbott facilities, 191; collaboration with George T. Rockrise & Associates, 189; commercial area, 194, *197;* design team, 189; and environmental concerns, 190, 199; Great Meadow, 194–96, *195,* 198; housing types and clusters, 191, *193,* 196–98; lagoon bridge, *190;* and landscape matrix concept, 48, 189,

196, 198–99; long-term plan and portion constructed, *188,* 190–91, 198–99; main lodge and deck, 191, *192, 196;* nature reserves and areas, 196–98; parks, 194, *194,* 198; planned facilities, 190–91, 194; planting plan, 198; riverfront preservation area, 194, *195;* Royston's role in, 189; separate road and pedestrian/bicycle path system, 196–98, *197, 198;* site history, 181, 191; site plan, *188,* 196–98; underpasses, 198, *198*

Sunset magazine: and California lifestyle, 22; Chinn garden in, 116: Royston and Stein gardens in, 75

Sun Yat-sen statue (Beniamino Bufano) in St. Mary's Square, *30,* 143, *144,* 146–48

SWA (Hideo Sasaki, Peter Walker, and Associates), 38

Swift, Florence Alton (artist), sculptural tiles in Royston garden, 78, 83

Taiwan, flood control projects in, 50

Takada, Hiko (architect), and San Joaquin Delta College design, 202–3

Taman Kiara National Arboretum (Kuala Lumpur, Malaysia), 50

Telesis group, 17, 71

Tetlow, Robert, at UC Berkeley Department of Landscape Architecture, 28

texture, use of: in Central Park (Santa Clara) chain arbor, 155; in Chinn garden paving, 112, 116; in Estates Reservoir

cover, 184; in Harris garden plantings, 231; and Kepes's *Language of Vision,* 26; in Mitchell Park plantings, 136; in plantings, 7; in Royston and Stein gardens, 76; in second Appert garden, 109; and spatial understanding, 54; in St. Mary's Square plantings, 149; in study models, 27

Thacher School (Ojai, CA), RHBA master plan for, 44–45; Church and, 44

Trachsel, Alfred (architect and planner), and playground design, 34

Tunnard, Christopher, *Gardens in the Modern Landscape,* 12

University of California, Berkeley, Engineering Building, RHBA site plan for, 211

University of California, Berkeley, Landscape Design program, 11–14; becomes Department of Landscape Architecture, 27–28; faculty, 28; Royston teaches in, 26–27, *28,* 31

University of California, Berkeley, Lawrence Radiation Laboratory (now Lawrence Livermore National Laboratory), RHBA development plan for, 33, 47

University of California, Berkeley, Royston's designs for, 32–33

University of California, San Francisco Medical Center, RHBA design for, 46

University of California, San Francisco, School of Dentistry, RHBA site plan for, 211